MW01148519

ADVANCED STICK FIGHTING

ADVANCED STICK FIGHTING

Masaaki Hatsumi
Translated by Bruce Appleby and Doug Wilson

KODANSHA INTERNATIONAL
Tokyo • New York • London

NOTE FROM THE PUBLISHER:
This book is presented only as a means of preserving a unique aspect of the heritage of the martial arts. Neither the publisher nor the author makes any representation, warranty, or guarantee that the techniques described or illustrated in it will be safe or effective in any self-defense situation or otherwise. Readers may be injured if they apply or train in the techniques illustrated. To minimize the risk of injury, nothing described in this book should be undertaken without personal and expert instruction. In addition, a physician should be consulted before deciding whether to attempt any of the techniques described. Federal, state, or local law may prohibit the use or the possession of any of the weapons described or illustrated in this book. Specific self-defense responses illustrated in these pages may not be justified in any particular situation or applicable under federal, state, or local law. Neither the publisher nor the author makes any representation or warranty regarding the legality or appropriateness of any weapon or technique mentioned in this book.

Jacket photos and most step-by-step photos by Kyuzo Akashi; some step-by-step photos by Naoto Suzuki.

Distributed in the United States by Kodansha America, Inc., and in the United Kingdom and continental Europe by Kodansha Europe Ltd.

Published by Kodansha International Ltd., 17-14 Otowa 1-chome, Bunkyo-ku, Tokyo 112-8652, and Kodansha America, Inc.

ISBN-13: 978-4-7700-2996-6
ISBN-10: 4-7700-2996-9

First edition, 2005
12 11 10 09 08 07 06 05   10 9 8 7 6 5 4 3 2 1

www.kodansha-intl.com

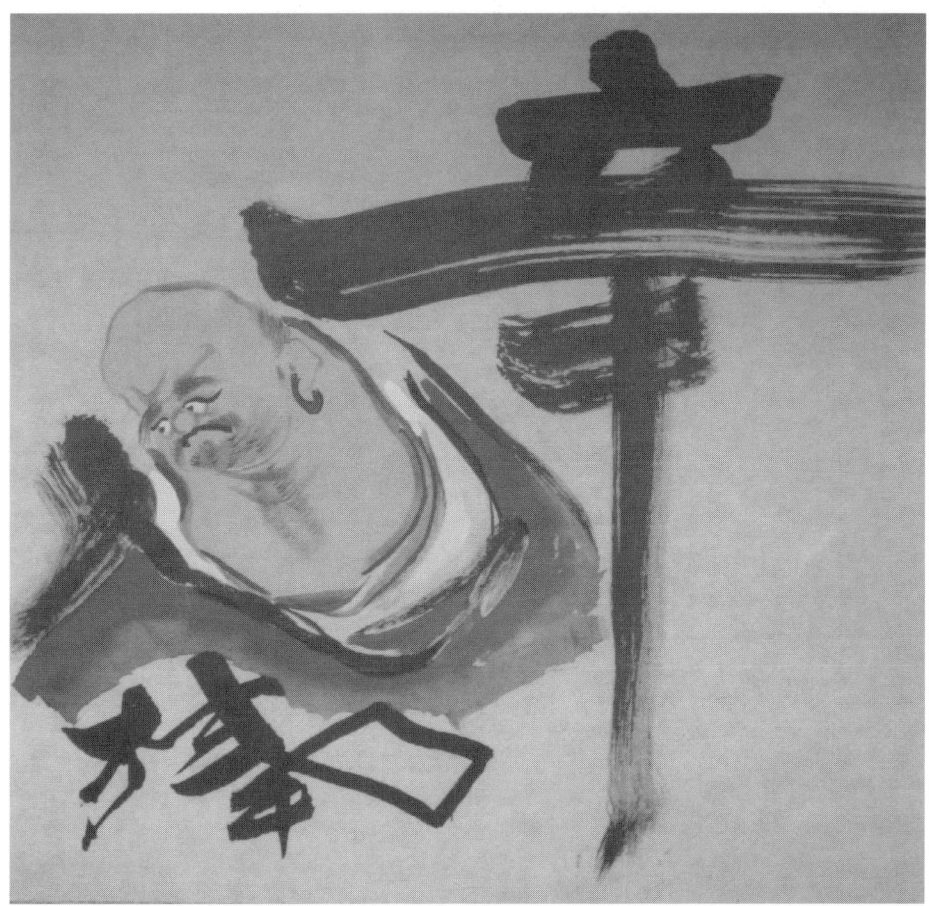

Shinbō (by Takamatsu Toshitsugu Sensei)

CONTENTS

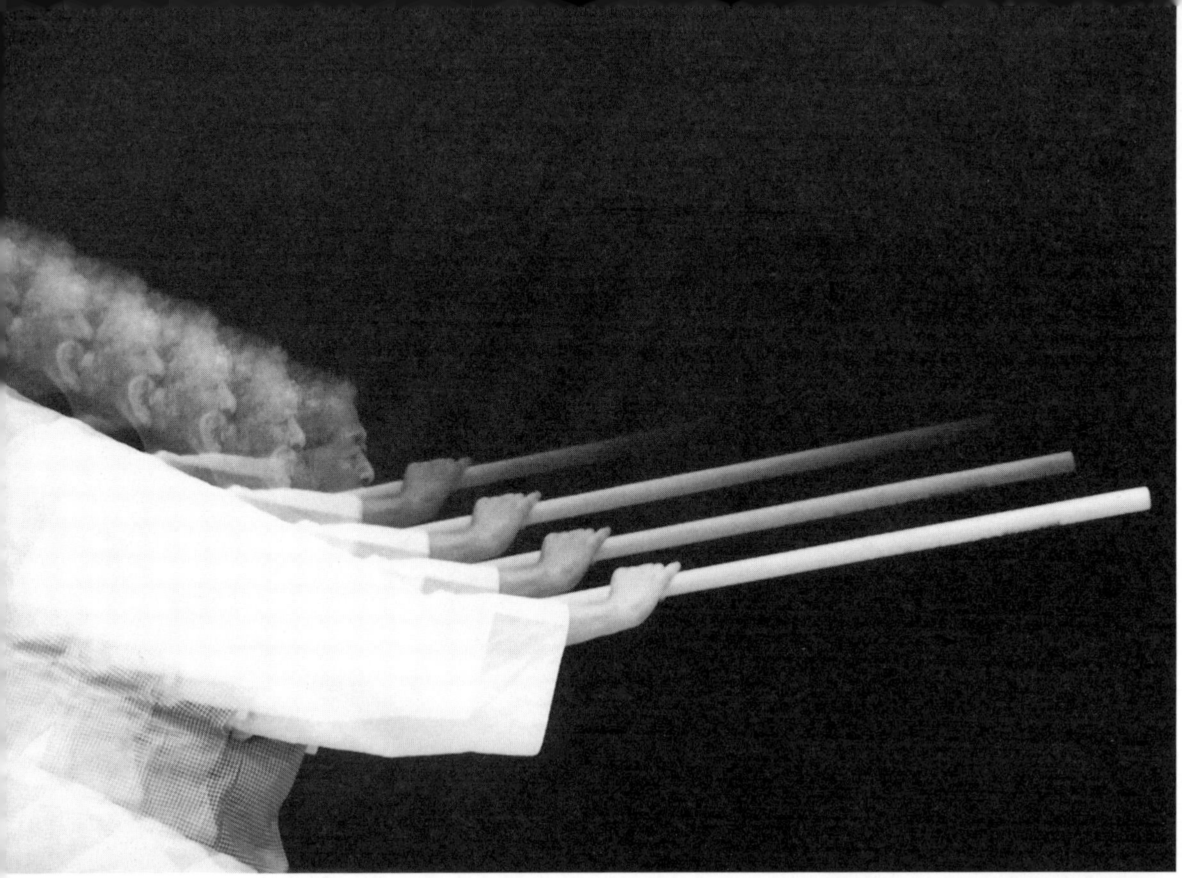

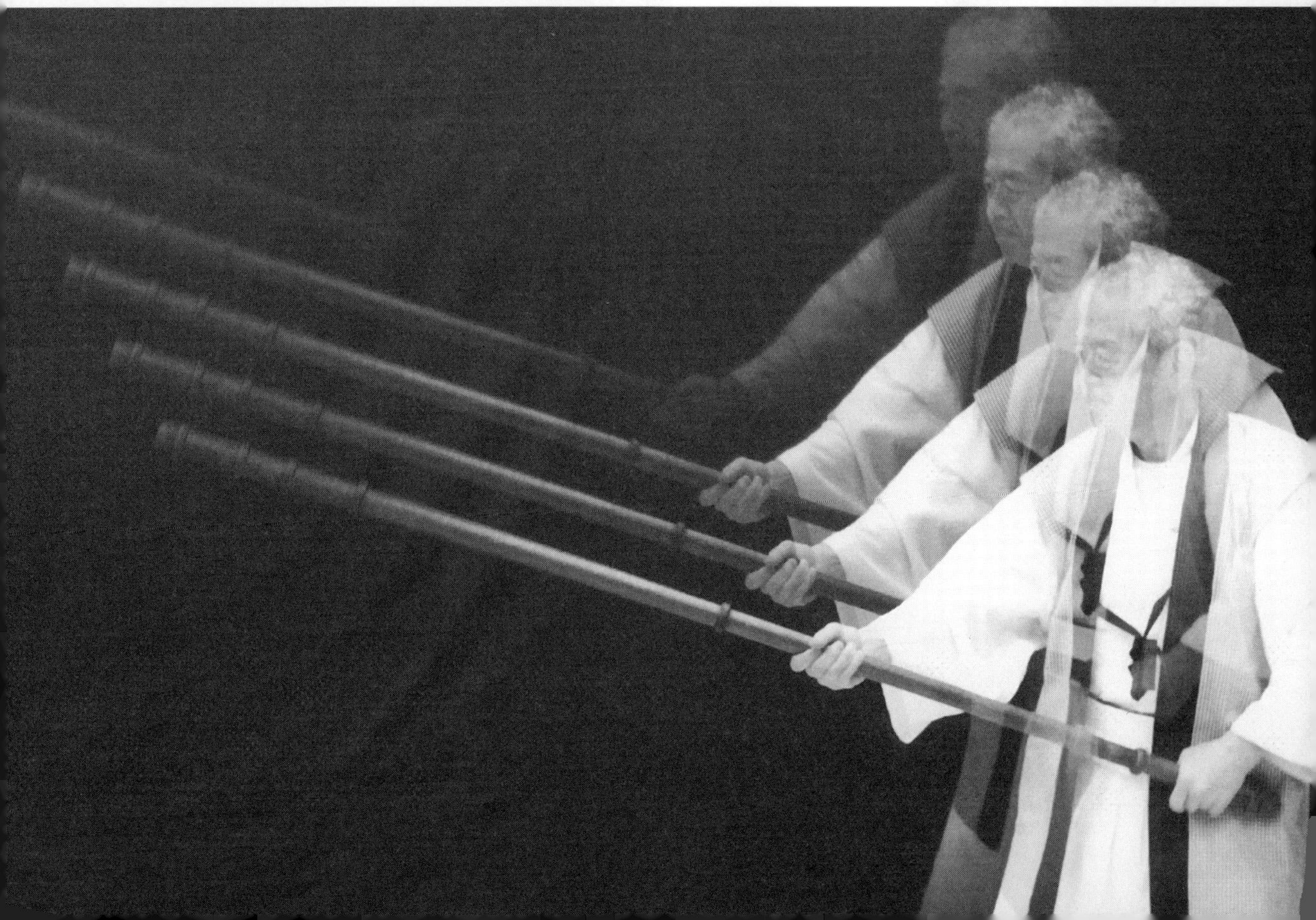

Kusanagai no Tsurugi (The Grass-cutting Sword used by Yamato Takeru no Mikoto)

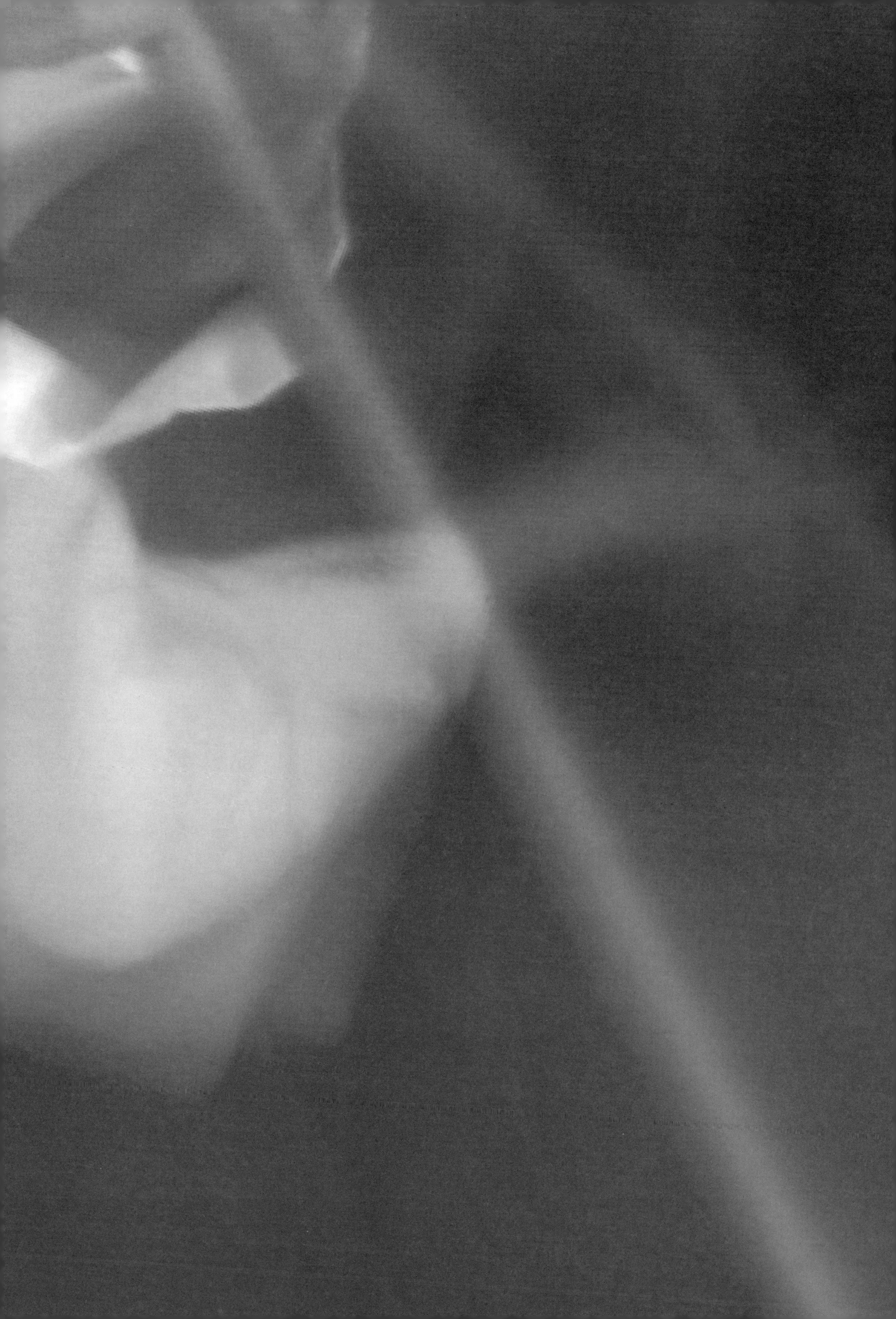

CHAPTER 1

The Essence of Budō is in Bō-jutsu

Bō-jutsu and Budō

Muga (selflessness)

Before using the word "Bushidō"

The Japanese term "bushidō" means "the way of the warrior." A famous warrior who achieved great renown was Taira no Kiyomori (1118–1181). Until Kiyomori's time "bushi (武士)," otherwise known as samurai (侍), were regarded, as the Chinese characters suggest, as "those who served," and were forbidden from entering the imperial court other than in exceptional circumstances. There is a saying: "one art relates to all others." Kiyomori was a general who also climbed to the post of Chief Minister of the Government, and helped manage the country politically, thereby demonstrating a multi-faceted sense of both warrior and samurai. He excelled as a strategist and was skilled at both assembling and commanding an army in combat. He also possessed political power and, at the same time, the economic means to maintain an army. Political power is not confined to a simple awareness of tactics, rather, the ability to see beyond the present is far more important. Other leaders who later held power in Japan, such as Oda Nobunaga (1534–1582) and Tokugawa Ieyasu (1542–1616), also possessed the foresight to see the future.

The sense of knowing, or intuition, is the first point within the essence (gokui) of budō. Reaching this point means one has attained the ability to prophesize the future, like a sage or a saint. The essence of fighting also demands the ability to foretell the future. In budō, the symbol of foresight is the tiger. The tiger suggests the power to foretell, infer, and see through phenomena and people; and survive by not being concerned with immediately trivial matters. I believe, in this time of suffering from war and rivalry, this ability is more important than ever. Moreover, what is important is not physical or conscious foresight, but inference and foresight based on subconsciousness or "ultra-consciousness," and responding to signs. Sometimes simply sitting and carefully observing is the best way to attain this foresight. However, there are very few people who can enter this state of "ultra-consciousness."

Normally, these select few would be called "geniuses," but "genius" in another sense means changing into something other than human. Genius (tensai) doesn't mean, as the characters suggest, a divine ability (tensai; 天才), but the ability to change (tensai; 転才). For example, to change freely into either an insect or animal according to necessity. Insects, animals, and plants are capable of foreknowledge, and only by sharing this sense of foreknowledge can we connect to a divine consciousness. Indeed, from this, the forces of natural power and reincarnation are born. In other words, the "genius" to change is a natural conscious-

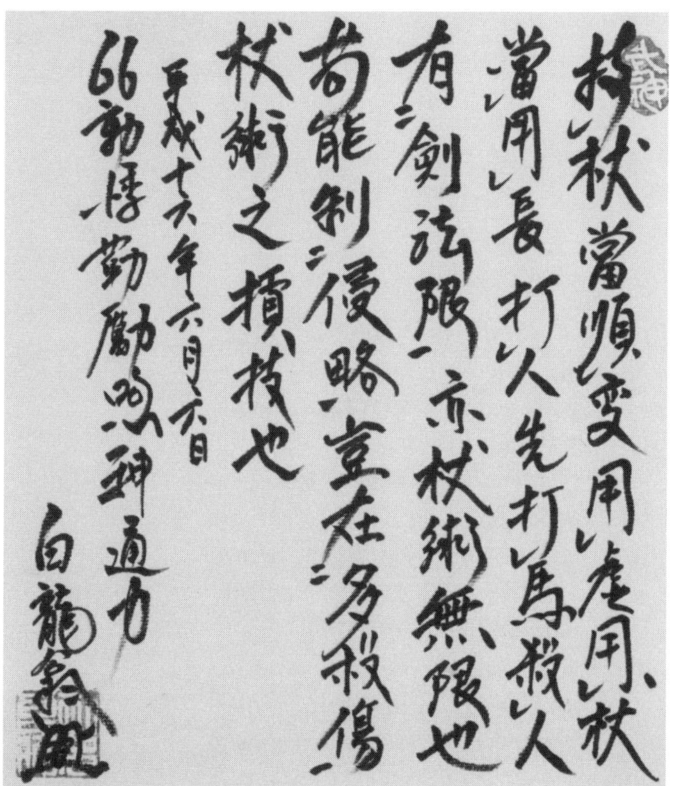

Regarding principles of the Jō

From Pope Paulo to the Author

ness, or ultra-consciousness, that exceeds humankind. Martial artists seek to develop this "changing genius." This is known as Tenchijin san sai no hō—the law of the three abilities of Heaven (ten; 天), Earth (chi; 地), and Man (jin; 人).

This ability can be developed to a certain extent through training and practice. However, training in itself, even for many years, does not guarantee achieving this level. Furthermore, even attaining Tenchijin san sai no hō does not make one impervious to tragedy and misery. After warrior Kiyomori's death, for example, the two children of an enemy commander whose lives he had spared later returned to murder his entire family.

This episode, as recorded in the *Heike monogatari*, echoes the truth of the saying that "all things are transient." Within budō there are five morals: jin-gi-rei-chi-shin. These five cardinal virtues start with benevolence. With alternative characters the five cardinal virtues (gojō; 五常) can also be expressed as the five mercies (gojō; 五情). But only the most capable warriors were able to control themselves and firmly push aside the human tendencies of altruism and kind-heartedness, thus allowing them to survive in battle and establish their name. Without this they could not bring about good fortune. We must remember, however, that this is just one of many aspects in the flow of time.

This ultra-consciousness (chō-kankaku; 超感覚) can also be understood as infinite consciousness (chō-kankaku; 逃感覚). By adding the kanji radical "shinyō" to "chō" (the character for infinite), the meaning then becomes to escape or avoid. The character "chō" implies the sense of defense, escape, and evasion, which are important in Ninjutsu.

It must, however, be recognized that it is difficult for a commander who lacks compassion, mercy, or benevolence to gain trust or popularity. The founder of the Kamakura government, Minamoto no Yoritomo (1147–1198), for example, has become infamous in history for taking the life of his younger brother Yoshitsune after he did not fully obey him. Oda Nobunaga's retainer, Tokugawa Ieyasu, was ordered by his lord to force his eldest son Nobuyasu to commit seppuku, a ritualistic suicide. This act of forced loyalty formed the basis of the three-hundred year rule of the Tokugawa shogunate. Though through this act Ieyasu was deified and consolidated tremendous power, his reputation was irreparably damaged. Despite pronouncing "forbearance is the basis of eternal peace and security, think of anger as your enemy," he was reviled as a merciless ruler.

Know natural posture

Many people who read Daidōji Yūzan's (1639–1730) *The Code of the Samurai*, Yamamoto Tsunetomo's (1659–1719) *Hagakure*, sword master Miyamoto Musashi's (1584–1645) *Book of Five Rings*, or literature related to these works, believe that bushidō is a remarkable philosophy. Certainly, reading words like "the way of bushidō is death" in Hagakure, or "no regrets in what I do" in Musashi's *Dokkodo*, is sure to induce a certain sense of awe regarding bushidō. However, personally, I think these essays are little more than a random

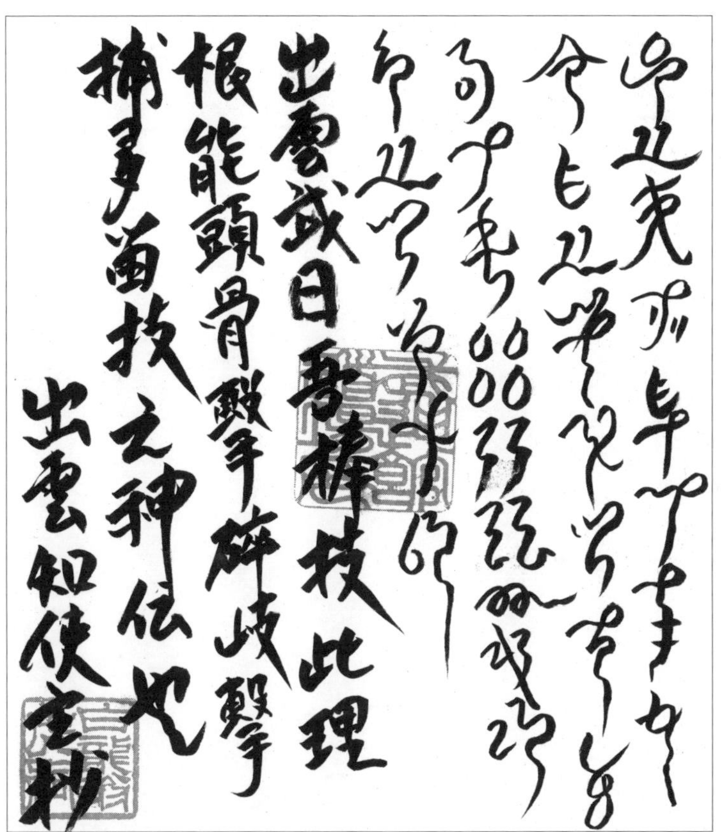

Regarding the history of the Jō

英雄六家撰
山本勘介入道道鬼齋
一勇齋
國芳画
横川

◀ Yamamoto Kansuke—swordsman and military commander, picture by Utagawa Kuniyoshi

collection of writers' notes or reflections. Unfortunately, their writings, Musashi's included, demonstrate that they did not reach the highest level in martial arts, and their experiences and writings are mere illusion. In this sense, they are like Jean Renoir's famous work "The Grand Illusion," or Stroheim's "Foolish Wives."

What I urge people to understand here is that the so-called essence (gokui) should not be regarded as the peak of the mountains, rather it is more like the flat of the plains. Gokui means to lead an ordinary life, it is to possess an "everyday mind" (heijōshin), and it is naturalness epitomized. All this is captured in the phrase "Bufū-ikkan," which in one interpretation means the permanence of the martial arts. It is for these reasons I constantly say that if you are always seeking gokui, you will loose its very essence.

The current surge of interest in bushidō is in many ways a search for an illusional world. Now that medieval notions of chivalry no longer have the same meaning in modern society, many people, including martial artists, pursue a fantasy of bushidō, rather like Cervantes's famous literary character Don Quixote. However, from here some people emerge who are drawn to the true immortal values of bushidō and to real martial arts.

In budō there are "outer" and "inner" techniques (known as "ura" and "omote" respectively). More than the mystery of the "oneness of the outer and inner," one must understand the mystery of change (tenkan; 転換), or rather the divine insight (tenkan; 天勘) to see between truth and falsehood (kyo-jitsu; 虚実). Tai-jutsu (body alignment; 体術), for example, has two aspects–one is illusion, but it can also be said to be "miraculous truth" (tai-jitsu; 妙実).

Natural power (this can also be written as natural mystery or natural posture) is of great importance in bushidō. There are people like my teacher Takamatsu Toshitsugu (1889–1972) who, living plainly each day, learn an "ultra sense," and survive through many chaotic situations. As a military man, to serve one's country, to serve one's lord, or to die for an ideal is important. But something that transcends this is to protect one's country, protect one's lord, and to attain an ideal. This is the true essence of the warrior, and what flows there is the real bushidō.

A person who can stay behind the scenes, who can remain influential in the corridors of power, but out of public scrutiny, can erase the "self." They can remain in the shadows, pursue good, and live simply. Martial artists and politicians alike seek to do this in various ways. For example, Ieyasu often consulted the High Buddhist Priest Tenkai (1536–1643), whom he had entrusted as his adviser. Tenkai influenced Ieyasu from behind the scenes and was secretly called the "Prime Minister in black." Koga Masao (1904–78), a leading popular songwriter, wrote a song entitled "Yearning for the shadows." This song has become well known and highly acclaimed, and has been said to express the very heart of Japan.

It is considered good manners to "walk three feet behind one's teacher without stepping on his shadow." Positioning one's shadow as a shield against the opponent when in combat; in other words, hiding in sunlight, is the real shadow of budō. In Ninjutsu there is a word "ton'ei." This means "shadow shield;" casting your shadow forward.

There are many things and people in the world that are outwardly impressive but have no inner power; conversely, things that are more hidden often possess real power. An iceberg, for example, floats in the sea because the hidden part is very large. Hypothetically, if there was no ice submerged under the water it would not be possible to walk on the iceberg—it would sink.

Recently, I feel that there are people who have begun to seek seriously the real tradition of budō; namely budō without any illusions. True bushidō, which our ancestors spent their lives to protect and convey from generation to generation, is thinking, philosophy, religion, the basis of a way of life, wisdom of life, and, of course, fighting techniques. Bushidō has many remarkable aspects, but you cannot live or defend yourself without applying real bushidō to all aspects of your life. This is something I would like readers of this book to understand. To persevere in real bushidō you must learn self control.

Musha Shugyō

I visited New Jersey in America in the summer of 2003 to teach martial arts bringing to an end my global musha shugyō (martial training). I was also curious to learn more about some of the major problems facing the world today, like international terrorism, global warming, and environmental destruction, which I explored in many discussions with various people. When I returned, my doctor was amazed at my medical test results—my blood showed an extremely high blood-sugar level of 320 and hemoglobin of Ab–Alc 9.2. However, when I had a second test one month later, my blood-sugar level was 160 and hemoglobin 7.1. Why? Because I quickly returned to a Ninja lifestyle, leaving behind a Western diet, which includes large quantities of meat and alcohol. Upon

Musha shugyō: martial training. Picture of Minamoto no Yoshimitsu, swordsman and military commander

returning, I cut out salt and sugar, and followed a strict Ninja diet of tofu, sesame seeds, miso soup, and vegetables. I also ate brown rice cooked with red beans (azuki), black soybeans (kuromame), and shiitake mushrooms. Furthermore, I was careful not to eat so much that my stomach became full; the kihon happō of being 80% full. When your stomach becomes full, you relax physically and mentally and become unable to respond quickly. On my third check up, my blood-sugar had fallen to 130 and hemoglobin 5.9, returning to completely normal within two months. Despite being an old man of seventy-three, I was able to recover, and I realized again the importance of spiritual awakening. This is true musha shugyō.

I think it is good to push yourself to the extreme; to push your mind and body to the point of imminent death has a purpose during a time of war. The tradition of severe training (musha shugyō) in the martial arts aims to awaken inner power. However, when the appropriate time comes, change swiftly. This is "tenkan," in other words, being able to control yourself.

Living in the mountains or living an isolated lifestyle is not the original form of martial training. If you can control yourself, maintaining natural posture, your training place is here, right where you are. Real bushidō, then, is not something that happens in a far removed place. Takamatsu sensei often used to say "there are many real people who are not martial artists."

A weapon called the Bō

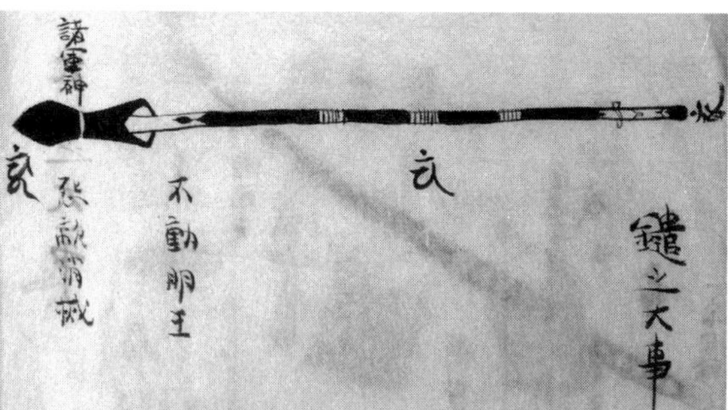

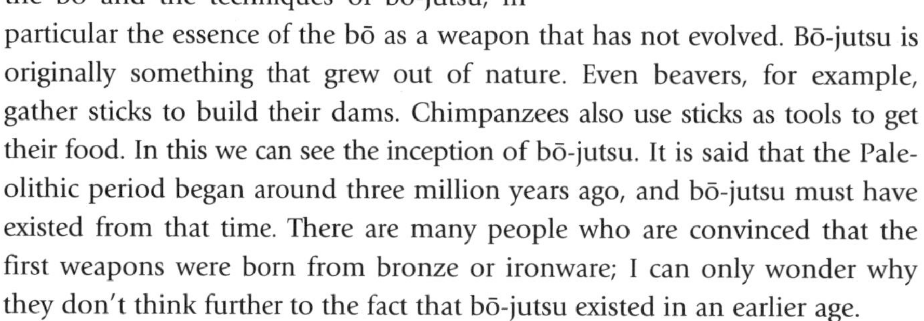

When did mankind begin to use weapons? Anthropologists say the earliest weapons were sticks and stones, as well as the bones of animals, and humans started making their own weapons during the Bronze Age. Historian Raymond A. Dart, for example, states that weapons preceded humans, and that our use of them fostered the evolution of man. According to another historian, in the last 5,000 years of human history, there have only been 280 years of peace. This means that there has been only 1 day in every 18 that is peaceful. It is very interesting that this number is the same as that of the 18 fields of martial arts (bugei-jūhappan), the samurai curriculum. When viewed this way, it would appear that the evolution and progress of mankind, which is considered to be positive by most people, is in fact quite disturbing.

I urge everybody to look again closely at the way humans live through the essence of the bō and the techniques of bō-jutsu; in particular the essence of the bō as a weapon that has not evolved. Bō-jutsu is originally something that grew out of nature. Even beavers, for example, gather sticks to build their dams. Chimpanzees also use sticks as tools to get their food. In this we can see the inception of bō-jutsu. It is said that the Paleolithic period began around three million years ago, and bō-jutsu must have existed from that time. There are many people who are convinced that the first weapons were born from bronze or ironware; I can only wonder why they don't think further to the fact that bō-jutsu existed in an earlier age.

Bō-jutsu can be found all over the world, varying in relation to climate and culture (particularly clothing). In Japan, an island nation and a country that was closed to the world during the isolationist policies of the Edo period (1600–1868), bō-jutsu became specialized during the course of history, and was protected and transmitted in secrecy, developing into a unique style.

What is Bō-jutsu?

Takahama Kyoshi (1874–1959), famous for his objective depictions of subject matter, wrote a haiku that portrays the attraction and essence of the stick:

The old year and the new—
Like a long stick
Continuing through.

Considering "the stick that continues through," I received a work of calligraphy by my teacher Takamatsu Toshitsugu that reads: "perseverance and consistency" (in this the character for perseverance is substituted with the character for bō). I keep this work in my reception room and whenever I view it, my heart is renewed. The history of this constant, perpetual stick represents the history of martial arts.

The first thing to know about bō-jutsu is that "the essence of martial arts is jūtai-jutsu (soft body arts) and the main weapons used are the stick and stone." Thus, bō-jutsu based on jūtai-jutsu is the origin of the martial arts. The true meaning of the "subtle arts" is to truly persevere. Incidentally, the word "to persevere" (taeru) can also be written as to "obtain many things" (taeru). As is generally accepted, the "kosshi" (backbone/core) of martial arts is body posture (kamae). It is essential one understands that what governs the kamae is the spirit.

Jūtai-jutsu is the basis, and only after learning this will you understand how to use a bō. The most important thing, in both bō-jutsu and ken-jutsu, is jūtai-jutsu. Without jūtai-jutsu, you cannot capture the true essence of the staff, nor will you be able to utilize it fully.

The densho (secret scrolls), passed down from Takamatsu Sensei, state "in the oldest records it is written that strategy (heihō) refers to five methods: daken-tai-jutsu, bō-jutsu, ken-jutsu, horse riding, and archery. With these protect and rule the country and be at ease in body." Also of significance is the following story regarding Miyamoto Musashi, known for "niten-ichiryū" (which means day sky and night sky): "It is said that Musashi only practiced sword fighting with two swords, but the disciplines Musashi-ryū bō-jutsu and Musashi-ryū dakenhō-taijutsu also exist, and were taught until the Meiji period. In this way the samurai, aside from strategy, would learn castle construction, sword, spear, and unarmed fighting, horsemanship, and stick fighting, as the martial arts.

A scroll showing Kukishin-ryū bō-jutsu painted by Takamatsu Sensei (The story is mentioned on pp.52-54)

In the infamous duel fought on Ganryū island, Musashi defeated Sasaki Kojirō, who was known for his skill in using a long sword of over 3-shaku in length, nicknamed "the clothes-drying pole." He won with a single blow from a sword he carved from the oar of the boat in which he sailed to the island. Musashi challenged his formidable enemy in a fight to the death, not with the two swords that he was best known for, but using the techniques of bō-jutsu, and took his opponent's life.

Sasaki Kojirō had been trained by his master in the short sword, but had become somewhat enamored of the long sword. It is important for readers of the many novels of samurai fiction to understand that there is a considerable difference between the world presented in these novels and the real world. For example, Kojirō is often depicted as similar in age to Musashi, when in fact he was much older. The above episode has made its way into legend, but it has been greatly dramatized by the novels.

Following the idea of the eighteen martial fields (bugei-jūhappan), Musashi was a master of various martial arts including jutte-jutsu, jō-jutsu, kyū-jutsu, and naginata-jutsu. Therefore, it was not necessary for him to rely solely on the sword even in a duel in which his life was in danger. Budō, partly because of the influence of Zen, often uses the phrases "throw away the body," "become naked," "become nothingness," but the secret to Musashi's victory over Sasaki is hidden in the fact that he was able to separate himself from his sword.

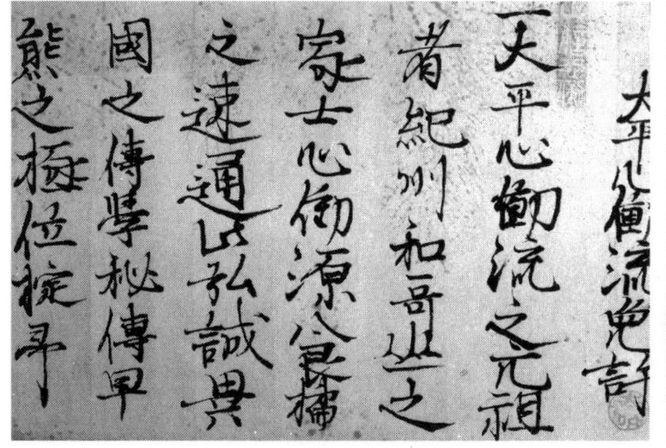

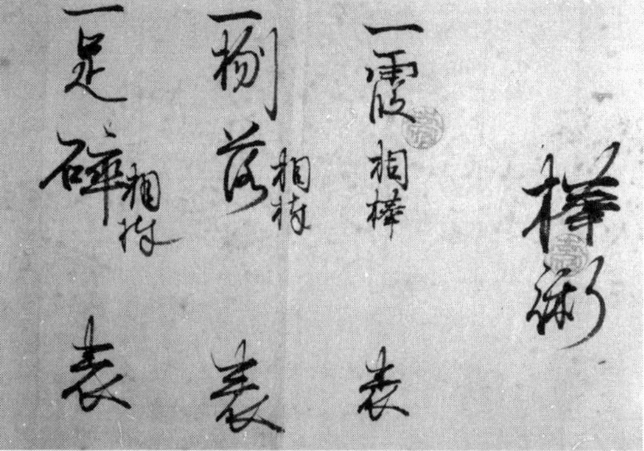

棒術
一霞　相棒　表
一柳蔭　相拵　表
一足碎　相拵　表

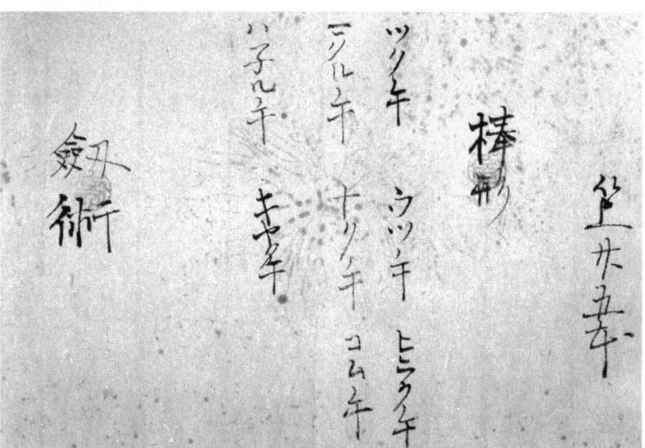

A bō-jutsu scroll of the Taihei Shindō-ryu

Fortunately, for his fighting skills at least, in addition to not being attached to his sword, he lived a life detached from women.

In one respect, however, this story is both lonely and sad. The reason for this is the history of humans can be summarized as:

1. The age of myth
2. The age of mono no aware; pathos
3. The age of wabi and sabi; elegant simplicity
4. The age of iki and inase; stylishness and chic
5. The age of mie; vanity
6. The age of mie mie; blatancy

Looking at the trends of the six ages that form the history of Japan we have the chance to reconsider the image of Musashi, especially the world of Musashi as portrayed by Yoshikawa Eiji.

The varieties of bō-jutsu

Techniques of the 6-shaku stick include the use of short sticks held in the hand and long sticks, of 8-shaku and over. Why are they called "6-shaku stick?" Before explaining, the first thing I encourage the reader to understand is the meaning of the five rings, as depicted, for example, in Musashi's "The Book of Five Rings." The five rings are earth, water, fire, wind, and void, and are intricately linked to many other philosophies. These include the go-gyō (五行) of wood, fire, earth, metal, and water; the five ways (五道); the ways of enlightenment (悟道); the five techniques (五術); the five teachings (五教); and the five cardinal virtues (五常-Jin-Gi-Rei-Chi-Shin). The number five is thus used to synthesize or unify a great variety of things. In Mikkyō, a sixth element—shiki (識)—exists in addition to chi, sui, ka, fu, and ku. In this way, "rokushaku" bō-jutsu refers not to the length of the stick but the six elements—rokudai. Therefore, the various different types of bō-jutsu should be looked at from the six-level worlds of Mikkyō with the six elements as "kasumi no hō." There are stories of mountain ascetics (sennin), represented by En-no-gyōja, who were said to be able to use mysterious powers and survive by eating only mist, having grasped the principle of eternal life. Reflecting on these stories, one will come to realize that they are crucial to the meaning of "kasumi no hō" of bō-jutsu, which is actually a teaching of the way (michi) for which you must grasp the six laws (this refers

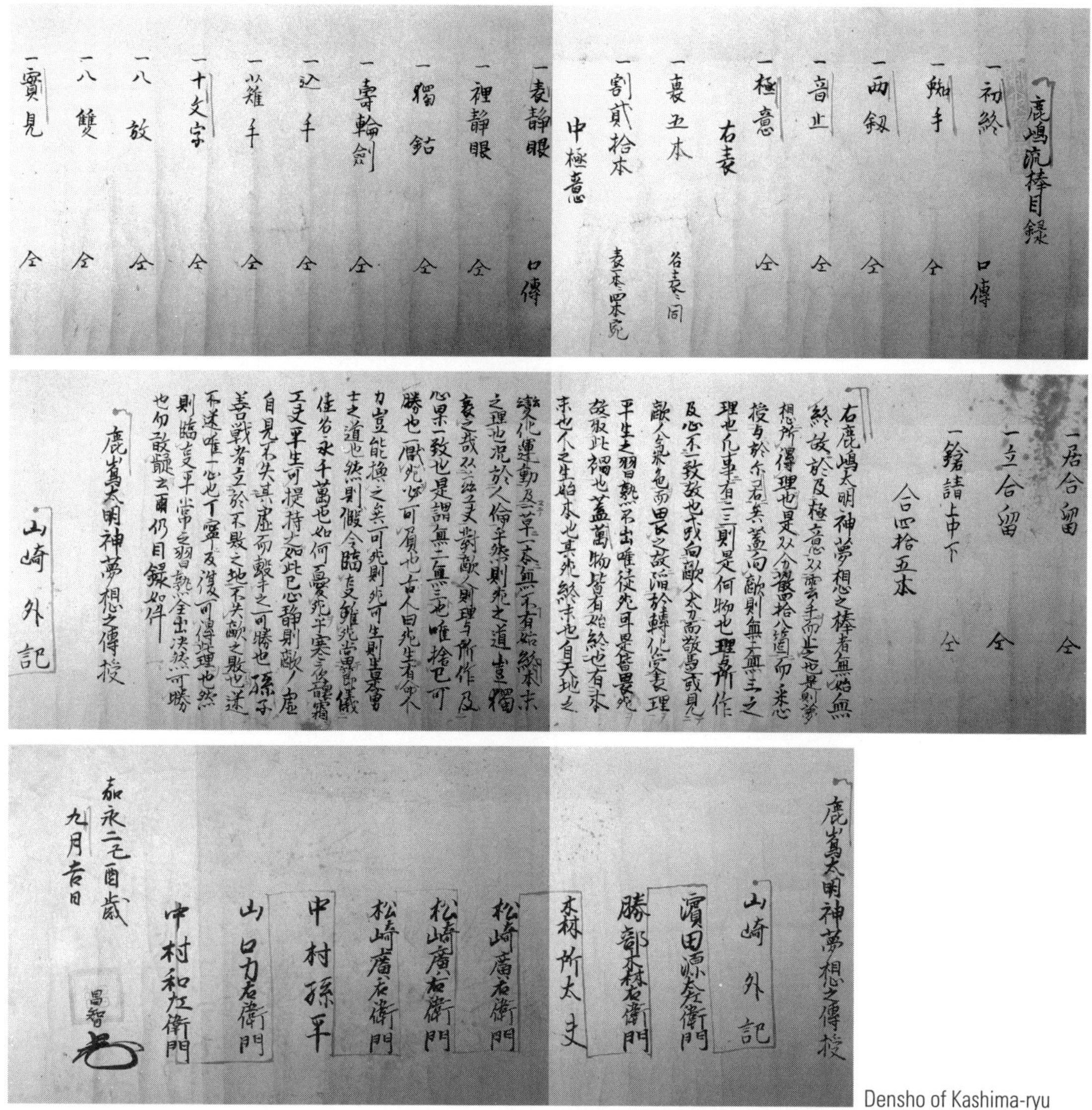

Densho of Kashima-ryu

to the compendium of Japanese law) of "the key point" (kanjinkaname). Those who fail to understand the meaning of six laws will never prosper.

Within hanbō-jutsu there are various techniques. In the technique Yanagi-ori, for example, an opponent holds your lapel and attacks. Applying omote gyaku with your left hand on the opponent's right hand, strike the opponent's chin with the end of the hanbō held in your right hand. Inserting the hanbō under the right arm of the opponent you throw the opponent, breaking his arm.

There are techniques using the jō instead of the bō. Bō-jutsu and jō-jutsu techniques using oak or loquat were also called "Kangi," or leverage techniques. In these, a red oak stick of 4-shaku 5-sun was used. The basis of leverage techniques is to be free to respond to the situation, taking advantage with deception. If you aim to strike the opponent, for example, first you strike the horse they are riding and then, taking advantage of this, you strike them.

The sound of the character for "stick" (Jō; 杖) is the same as that for "old man" (Jō; 尉). In Japanese traditional theater (Noh drama), the image of an old man suggests a world of elegant simplicity and subtlety (yūgen no sekai). Another character with the same sound (Jō; 情) means emotion or compassion. Thus, Jō-jutsu can be associated with truthfulness and sincere emotion (Jō-jitsu).

The bō or jō is stronger than certain swords that were sometimes chipped in real combat or broke when struck. The stick is a tool that allows you to defend yourself while avoiding killing or wounding an opponent. Amongst the types of bō, there are those which can be used to crush an opponent wearing armor, or the legs or back of a horse that they are riding, such as the Nyoi-bō.

The bō, however, had many uses beyond simply fighting. It could be used as a tool to enable one to scale walls or obstacles. It should also not be overlooked that the bō or jō was a religious symbol used from ancient times by priests to perform ceremonies. There is also the story of Moses who once threw his staff at an enemy, upon which it changed into a snake, frightening the opponent away.

We should look carefully at the character for "bō" (棒). It is comprised of the characters for "tree; 木" and "revere; 奉," thus meaning to "revere trees." The essence of the bō is related to prayer. Plants and trees absorb CO_2 within the atmosphere and produce oxygen, an important activity for the continuation of all life. This is truly a great process of change. The meaning of making the sword-stick from wood is contained within this idea.

The History of Bō-Jutsu

When did Bō-jutsu originate? According to Japanese legend, Susano no Mikoto set fire to the dry grass surrounding Ookuninushi no Mikoto in order to test him. Ookuninushi no Mikoto, picking up a stick, beat back the flames and prevented the fire from spreading. There is also the story of Izumo Takeru no Mikoto using a 3-shaku sword-stick to defeat his enemy. This

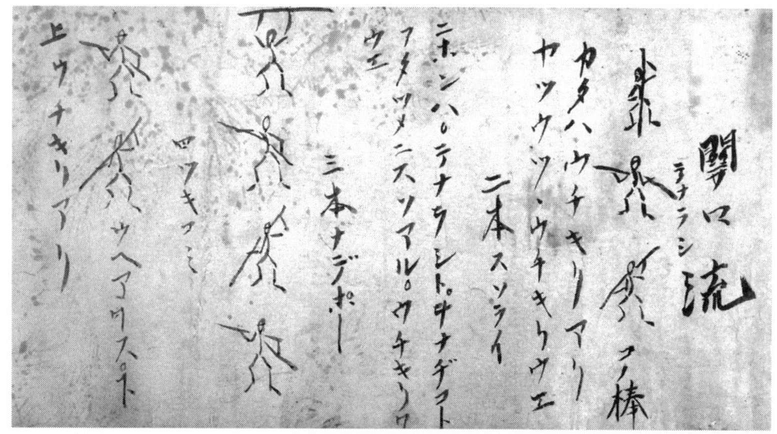

Densho of Sekiguchi-ryu

Kasumi (by the Author)

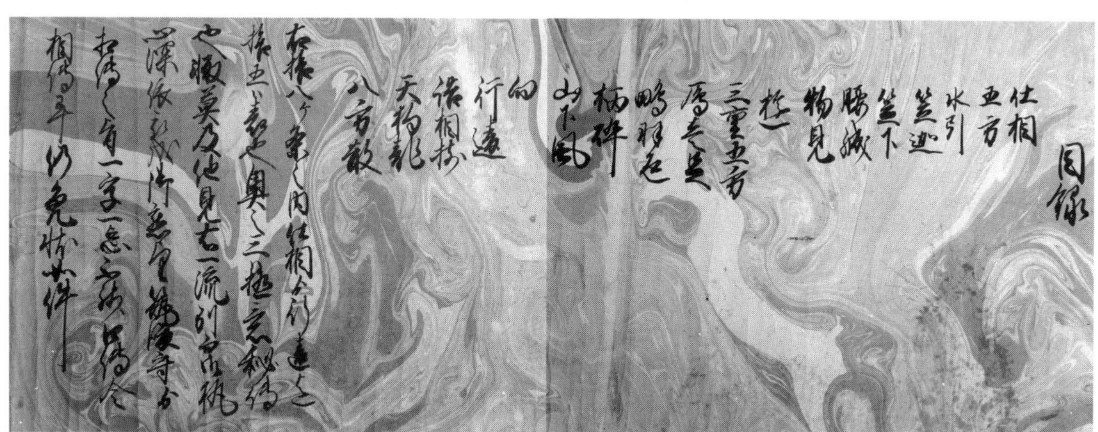

sword-stick was a weapon that only rulers could possess. Techniques of the sword, sword drawing, spear, and halberd were handed down from the techniques of the sword-stick and were further developed in later times. It is said that sword-sticks were around 3-shaku in length and were made using a strong wood from the local area with only the handle carved.

According to records within Kukushin-ryū, in ancient times, there was a weapon called a sword-stick of 3-shaku 5-sun with a stone ring attached to one end, and an 8-shaku stick with stone rings attached to both ends that were used to crush an opponent's head. In later periods, as warriors became more skilled in using the sword-stick and the 8-shaku stick, the stone ring was removed and the sword-stick was shortened to 3-shaku, evolving into hanbō-jutsu, stick-sword techniques, and jō-jutsu. And, of course, the stone rings were removed from the 8-shaku, and the bō-justsu of the 6-shaku stick was born.

According to records the oldest schools of bō-jutsu are Shinden-ryū, Kishin-ryū, Kumano-ryū, Kukishin-ryū, Happo-ryū, and Takagi-ryū. In later years, according to records in the densho of Katabami bizen no Kami, master of Ittō-ryū and a founder of Suwa-ryū, the principles of leverage (bō-jutsu) enable "one strike, certain kill."

In the scrolls of the schools of which I am a grandmaster, it is recorded that in the third year of Engen (1338), when Ashikaga Takauji attacked Kyoto, Ookuni Taro Takehide, retainer of Yūki Chikamitsu, fought the famous Yashiro Gon no kami Ujisato of the Ashikaga army. As in the legend of the broken arrow in the closing days of the Warring States Period (1467–1568), bō-jutsu with "techniques of the broken spear" can be found in various records. The sword-stick is even recorded in the *Kojiki* and *Nihon shoki*. It has also been said: "Unless you have mastered the truth of the 3-shaku sword-stick, the principle of sword fighting (kenpo) will elude you."

History of the Kukishin-ryū Bō-jutsu

A historical account within Kukishin-ryū bō-jutsu reads as follows:
In the first year of Engen (1336) the Emperor Godaigo was being held at the Kazan-in residence by Ashikaga Takauji. When the loyal servants of the southern dynasty lead by Kusunoki Masashige were planning how to rescue the emperor, a Ninja of Kishū named Yakushimaru Kurando was present. Thereupon, Kurando, who had mastered the art of Ninpō and surpassed all others in bravery, was ordered to take on the heavy responsibility of rescuing the emperor. At that time Kurando was a handsome young man of sixteen and therefore disguised himself as a lady in waiting, and stole into the Kazan-in residence. Carrying the Emperor on his back he crept down the corridor, but was discovered by a small rank of ordinary soldiers.

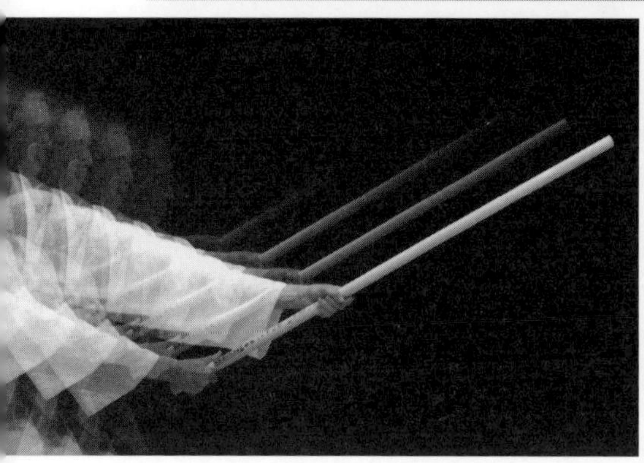

With a kiai he jumped down in front of the gate with the Emperor still on his back, and became surrounded by a general and his samurai from every direction. Putting the Emperor down in the shadow of a tree, Kurando took his naginata, known as Aranami, in one hand and shouted, "who is your leader?" As Kurando fought the enemy soldiers were cut down like grass.

However, the general's skill was not to be underestimated, and he cut the blade off Kurando's naginata. Kurando, quickly overcoming this disadvantage, applied the Ninja technique Roppō Kuji Kasumi no Hō, and fought ferociously. As he struck down the general, Kusunoki Masashige's troops arrived, and rescued the Emperor.

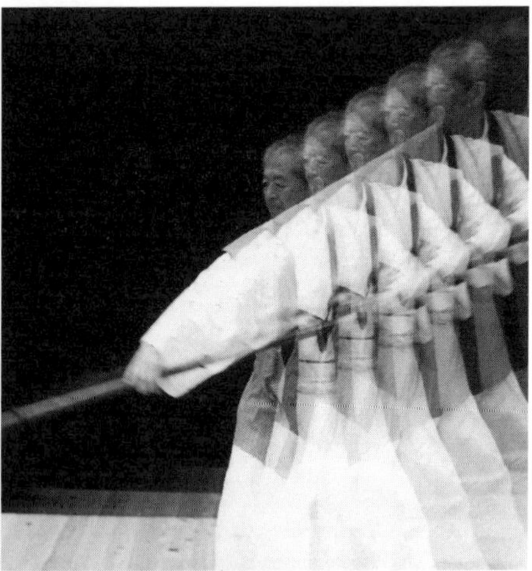

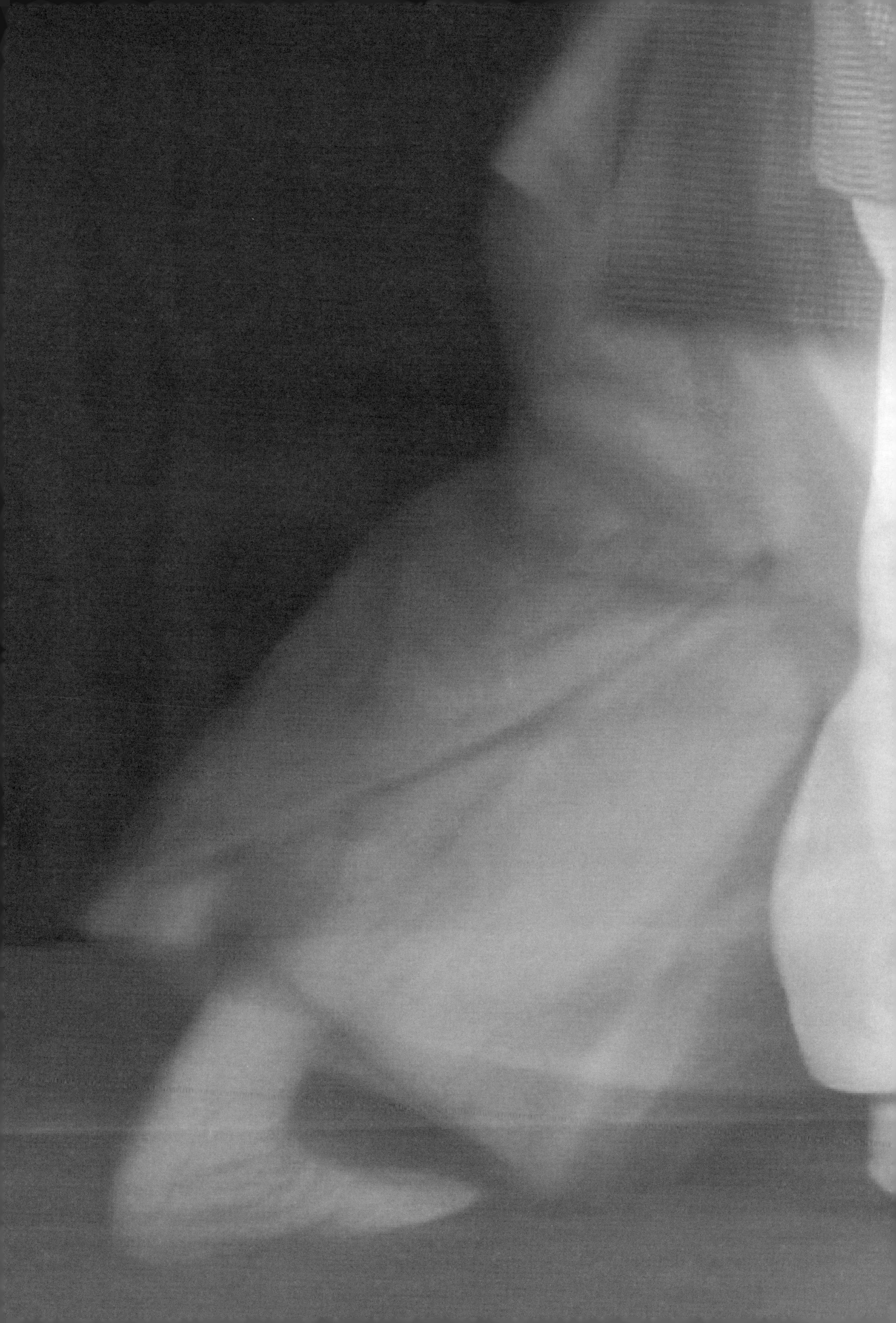

CHAPTER 2

The Practice of Bō-jutsu

The Divine Tune of the Breathing Bō

Un-a Kongō

The Quality of the Bō

The bō is deeply connected to the quality of the climate in which it grew, and the temperament of the holder.

When one decides to practice bō-jutsu it is also necessary to know about the quality of the stick. This is because the quality of wood differs according to the environment in which the tree grew. Just like recognizing a fine Masamune sword among many swords, you must train your eyes to be able to seek out an excellent stick. There are eight types of wood for a bō; this is the Kihon Happo of sticks. The most commonly used wood for the bō is that of the evergreen oak family, and within that family is the bō of red oak. These evergreen trees when fully grown can be up to twenty meters tall and one meter in diameter. The strength of the wood varies depending on the local environment. Red oak is a strong, hard wood, and has been used as handles for weapons since ancient times. Rough black oak, often used as hedging and in gardens, is a pale black color that appears to be dead, but is actually a wood with a very strong quality. It is said that within the oak family there are ten different varieties, including white oak. The "10" can represent jūmonji, or a cross, and implies a connection. It is very interesting that this is related to the Juppō Sesshō no Kamae introduced within Ninpō Tai-jutsu. Generally, it is considered best to cut evergreen oak from the equinoctial week (when Buddhist services are held) in September, until the first ten days of December. It is also fine to cut the wood when it is cold, but it could contain too much sap and be susceptible to infestation by insects.

After the evergreen oak, the next best example is the zelkova, which is strong and is used as a building material and for ornaments and utensils. Loquat is also a strong wood used for a jō, bokken, or naginata. Elm, often used for making kitchen utensils, is also fine. There are other sticks made from wood that is processed, hardening it to the strength of iron, sticks that are made of iron, and those like the shikomi zue, that have hidden swords within the wood. As in the saying "Just as Kukai didn't select his brush," it is important to understand one aspect of bojutsu is that you cannot always choose the quality of wood for your stick.

Bō breaks. The Way of Bushido is death.

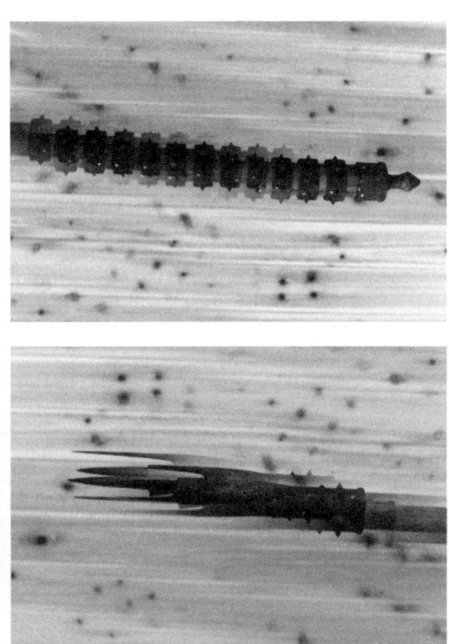

Types of Bō

Types of Jō

Bō Etiquette 棒の作法

Walk holding the bō in the center with the left hand. Change the bō to the right hand when you reach a distance of 6-shaku, kneel down in seiza and bow. Come to a half standing position with the right foot leading and stand the bō upright. both partners exchange the conventional expression "Ote yawaraka ni," which urges the opponent not to be too violent. Strike the bō firmly downwards. Lift the bō up with the right hand and move your left into place as you stand up and move into Kamae.

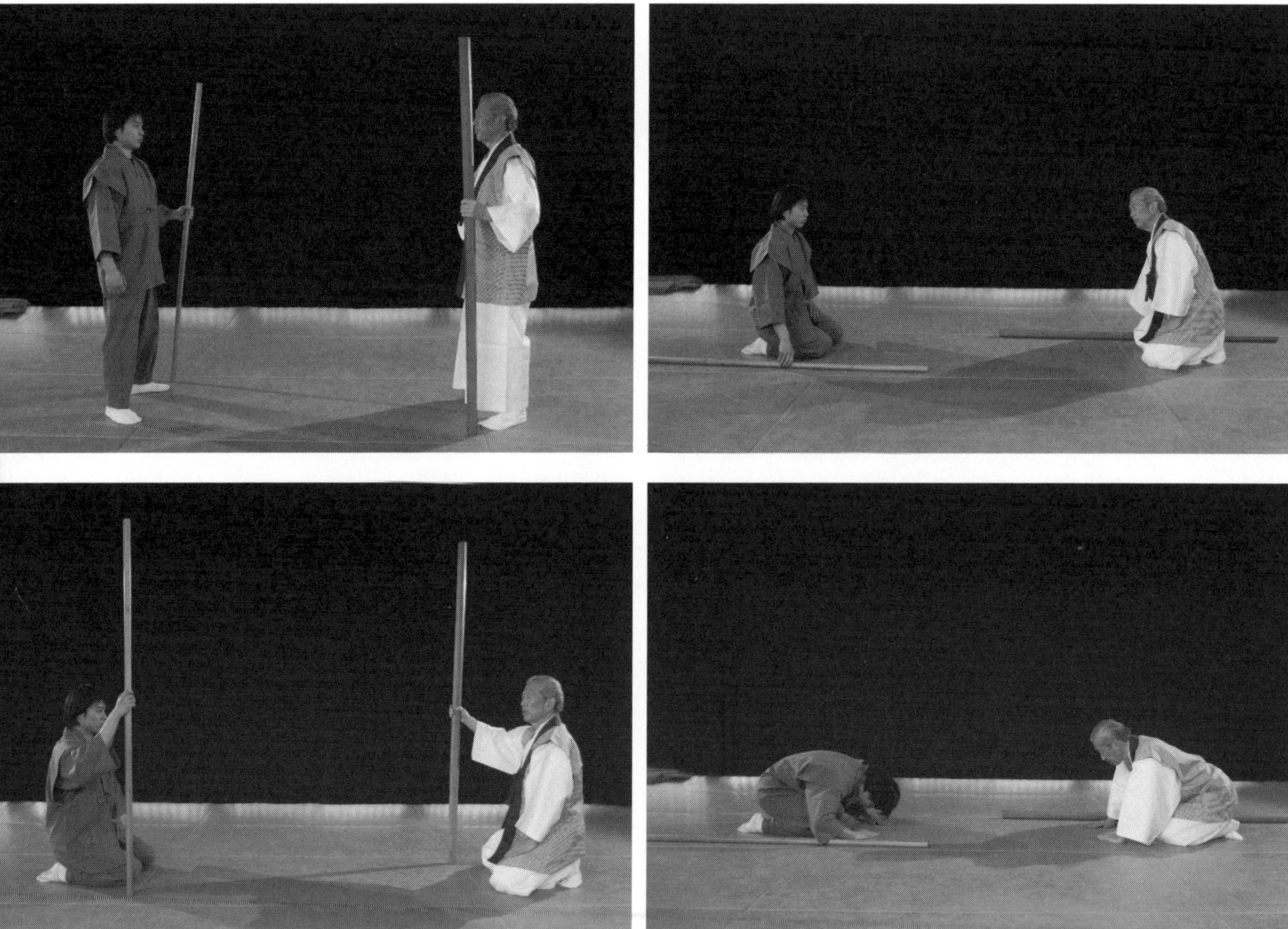

KISHIN KYŪHO NO KAMAE　奇神九法の構

Jōdan no Kamae　上段の構

Hold the bō in the middle with both hands facing downwards at a distance of 2-shaku apart. Preparing for movement (henka) with the left foot, place your center of gravity lightly on your right foot. The left foot should be forward and the right foot behind. Fix your gaze on the opponent's eyes and raise the bō above your head. Hold the right hand high in order to thrust into the opponent's eyes with the left end of the bō and lower the hips slightly. Your opponent should not be able to see your legs. This can also be called the "floating across" Kamae.

Chūdan no Kamae　中段の構

Hold the bō in the middle with both hands facing downwards at a distance of 1.5-shaku apart. Stand with your right foot behind, straighten your back, and round your chest. Straighten your left hand and put your right on the right-hand side of your chest. Hide behind the face of the end of the bō.

Gedan No Kamae 下段の構

Holding the bō in the center with both hands facing down at a distance of 1-shaku 5-sun apart, transfer your center of balance over the right leg, and rest the right end of the bō on the ground. Allow the face of the bō to act as a shield

Ichimonji no Kamae　一文字の構

Turn your body to the right and look directly forward. Hold the bō at the center with your hands facing down at a distance of about 2-shaku apart. The distance between your feet should also be 2-shaku. In this Kamae the stick is lowered to the waist level. This is also called Shigin In-Yo no Kamae

Hira Ichimonji no Kamae
平一文字の構

This is the same as Ichimonji no Kamae but the body faces directly forward.

Ihen no Kamae 誷変の構

The "I" in Ihen can also be read as "azamuku" and means to deceive. In other words, to lure the opponent by changing (henka). Place the left foot forward and the right foot back at a distance of 2-shaku. Maintain lightness in your center of balance over your right leg. Hold the bō in the center, balanced with both hands facing down. The left hand should be straight and the right hand near to the side of your head. This can also be called Koteki Ryoda no Kamae.

青眼

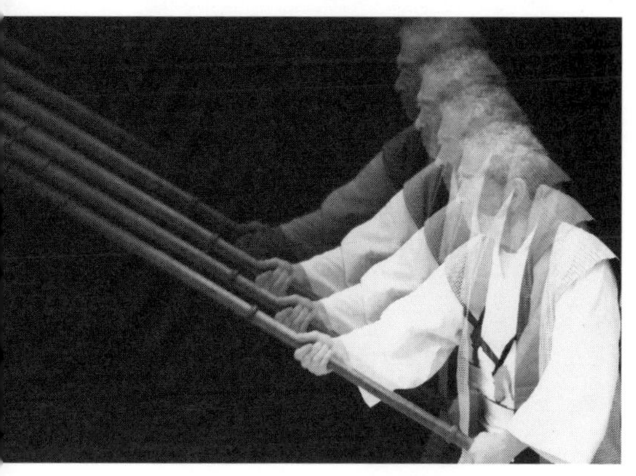

Seigan no Kamae 青眼の構

Place your right leg forward and left leg to the rear with a space of 1-shaku 5-sun. Hold the bō in the center with the hands 1-shaku 2-sun apart. Your right hand should face to the left and left hand to the right. The right hand should not be tense, and should be in direct line with your nose at a distance of 1-shaku 5-sun. The left hand should be placed in the region of the abdomen. This can also be called Kami Shin no Kamae

Ten Chi Jin no Kamae 天地人の構

Assume a right-facing posture with a distance of 1-shaku 2-sun between your legs. Hold the bō with both hands facing you. Hold the center of the bō with your right hand under the jaw with your elbow "rounded." Hold the left hand in the area of the abdomen. The distance between the hands should be 1-shaku 2-sun. Although it is taught that the bō should be held in the center, in practice it is held in a 60:40 (upper/lower) ratio. Hold the bō to your right side. This can also be called San Ryaku no Kamae.

Heitō no Kamae 撃倒の構

This Kamae is also known as Harai (to pay; also, to sweep). The left leg must be forward and the right leg pulled back at a distance of 1-shaku 2-sun. Hold the bō with both hands 2-shaku apart. Both hands should face downward. Pull the right hand back so the bō comes back behind you to the side. This Kamae is unsuitable for attacking, but is very effective when countering an opponent's attack. According to some traditions, this kamae is also known as Hannobanetsu no kamae.

Kihon Gata

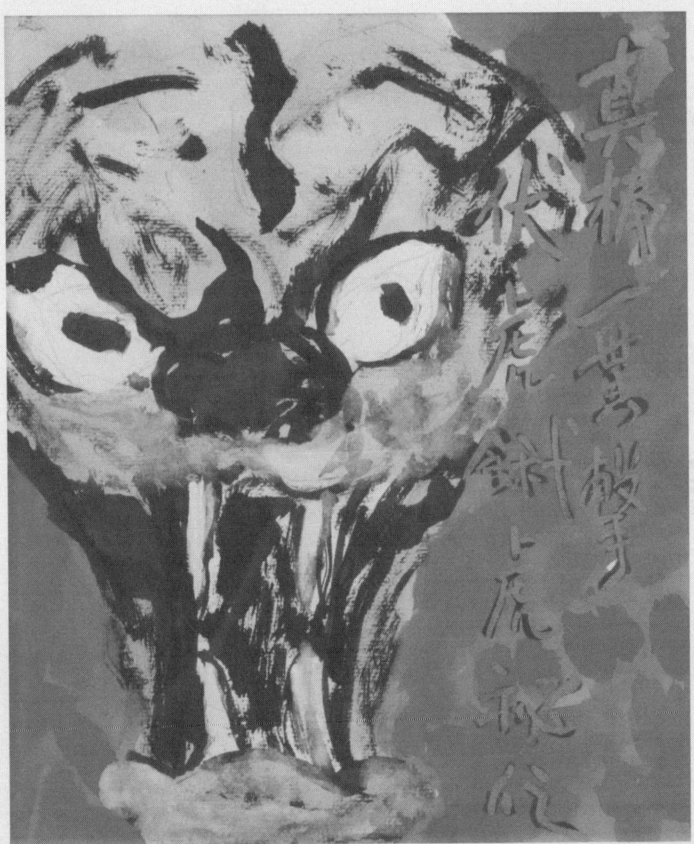

Gako Hiden

SHIRA KIHON GATA 四羅起本型

Ukemi 受身

Both opponents, on an east-west line of the dōjō, bow. both are in Hira Ichimonji no Kamae, at around 4-shaku distance.

The attacker takes a step forward with the right foot and strikes down to the top of the defender's head with the right end of the bō.

The defender, taking a step back to the left with the right foot, receives the strike, cradling the bō in the palm of the right hand. Lift the right hand approximately 3-sun above the head with the elbow in the direction of the tip of the bō. Lift the left hand, which is used lightly, straight up above the head on the left side. As the opponent's stick comes down on your head, it is received by the bō in a diagonal position.

With this type of defense, even if the opponent's weapon were a katana it would be difficult for them to cut the bō in two. Because the fingers of the defender's right hand do not reach above the bō, even if the blade slipped, the fingers would not be cut. The bō, supported by light use of the forearm, is a strong defense. It is important that the body is sufficiently arched backwards.

Ashi Barai 足払

As before, start in Hira Ichimonji no Kamae. The opponents are at a distance of 4-shaku apart. The attacker takes a step forward and strikes left ashi barai with the right end of the bō. At the same time, the defender reacts by striking with ashi barai in the same way. However, because the defender's movement occurs a fraction later, he steps back with the left leg and strikes to the attacker's left leg with ashi barai. The attacker's bō and defender's bō strike and receive in the same motion.

The attacker releases the right hand, rotates the stick over, and again strikes with ashi barai. The defender releases the left hand and, rotating the bō, receives the attack.

From this position, the attacker strikes right ashi barai with the left end of the stick. When doing this, he lets the bō move a little to the left side. The defender, matching the movement of the attacker, steps back with the right leg and receives the attack.

The attacker then throws the right end of the bō upward and releases. He then strikes the opponent with ashi barai using that end of the bō. The defender receives the strike moving in the same way as the attacker.

Ashi Barai 足払

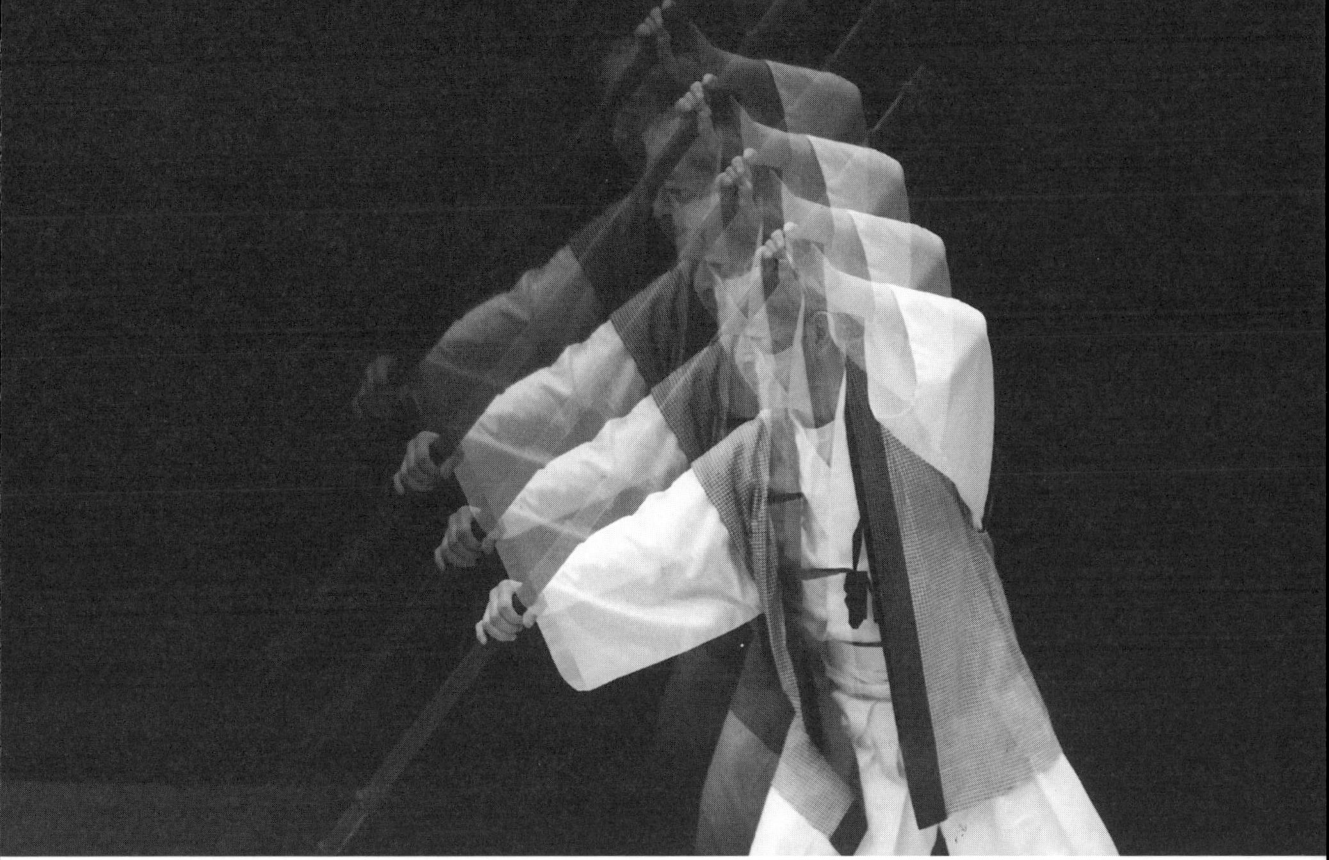

Ashi Barai 足払

Shihō Bōfuri Gata 四方棒振型

Holding the bō in the center, left hand up, right hand down, lean your body diagonally to the right and push the bō down with your right hand, rotating your left hand to face downwards. Holding the stick with your right hand facing downwards release your left hand. Turn the body to face left and push the bō down with your left hand, then release the left hand. When your right hand faces down, re-take the bō with your left hand facing downwards. Turn your right hand, and when your left hand faces up, take the stick with your right hand facing downward. Leaning your body to the right again, repeat the movement above. The bō will then spin, making a noise like a windmill. Spinning the hand-stick with just one hand is sometimes practiced, but this is not the correct method in bō-jutsu.

Men Uchiharai Gata 面打払型

Attacker and defender stand facing to the right holding the bōs with the left hand facing up and the right hand facing down. The attacker flips the bō with the left hand and strikes to the defender's left leg. From this position, the attacker strikes the side of the opponent's face. The defender responds by taking the same form as the attacker. The attacker moves the bō slightly to the left and strikes ashi barai from the same position, again hurling the bō up with the right hand, rotating, and striking the defender's left leg with the right end of the bō. The defender takes the same form to receive the attack.

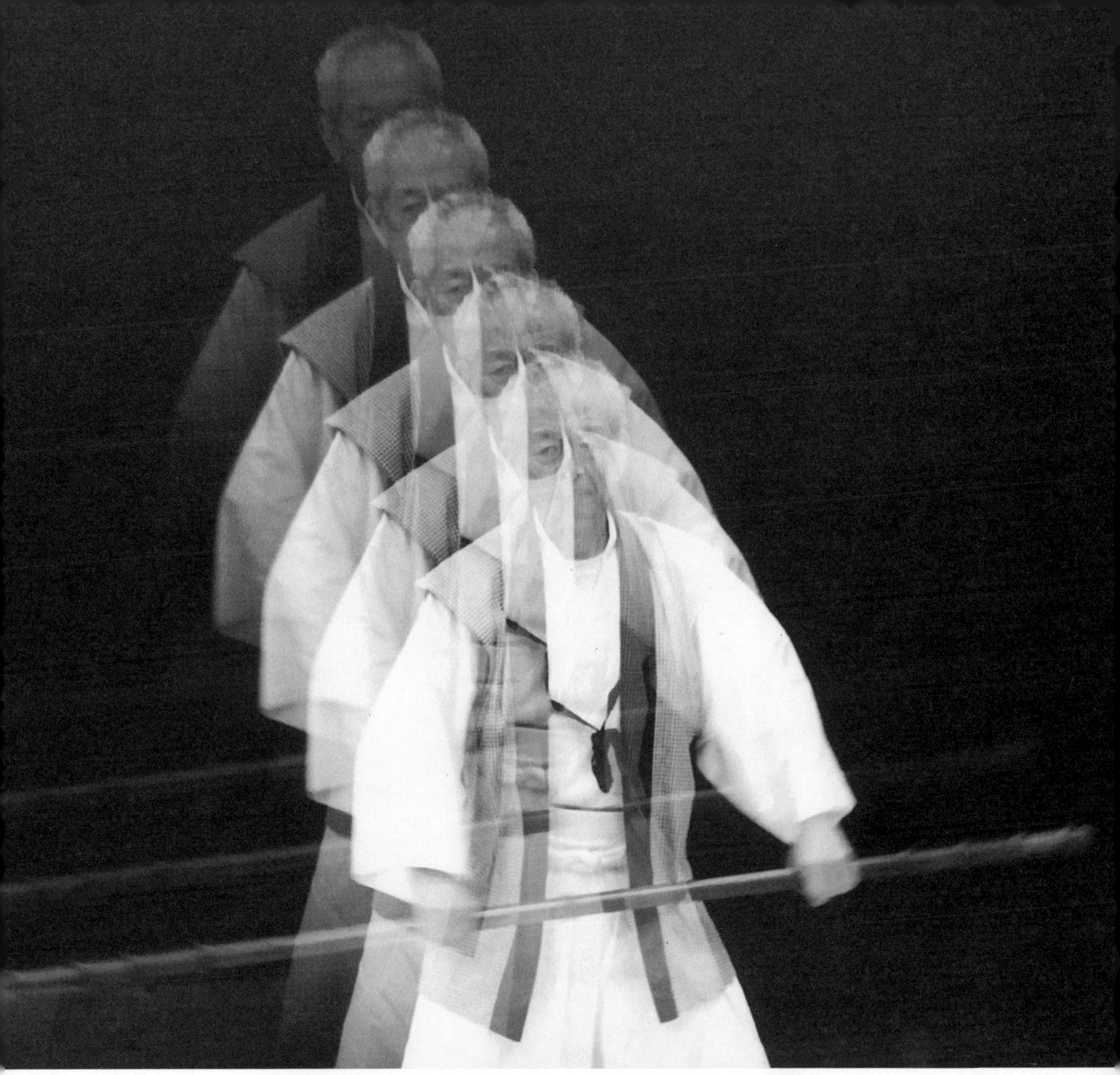

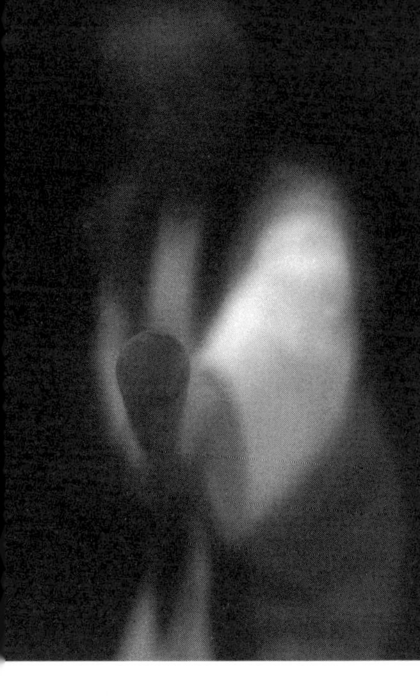

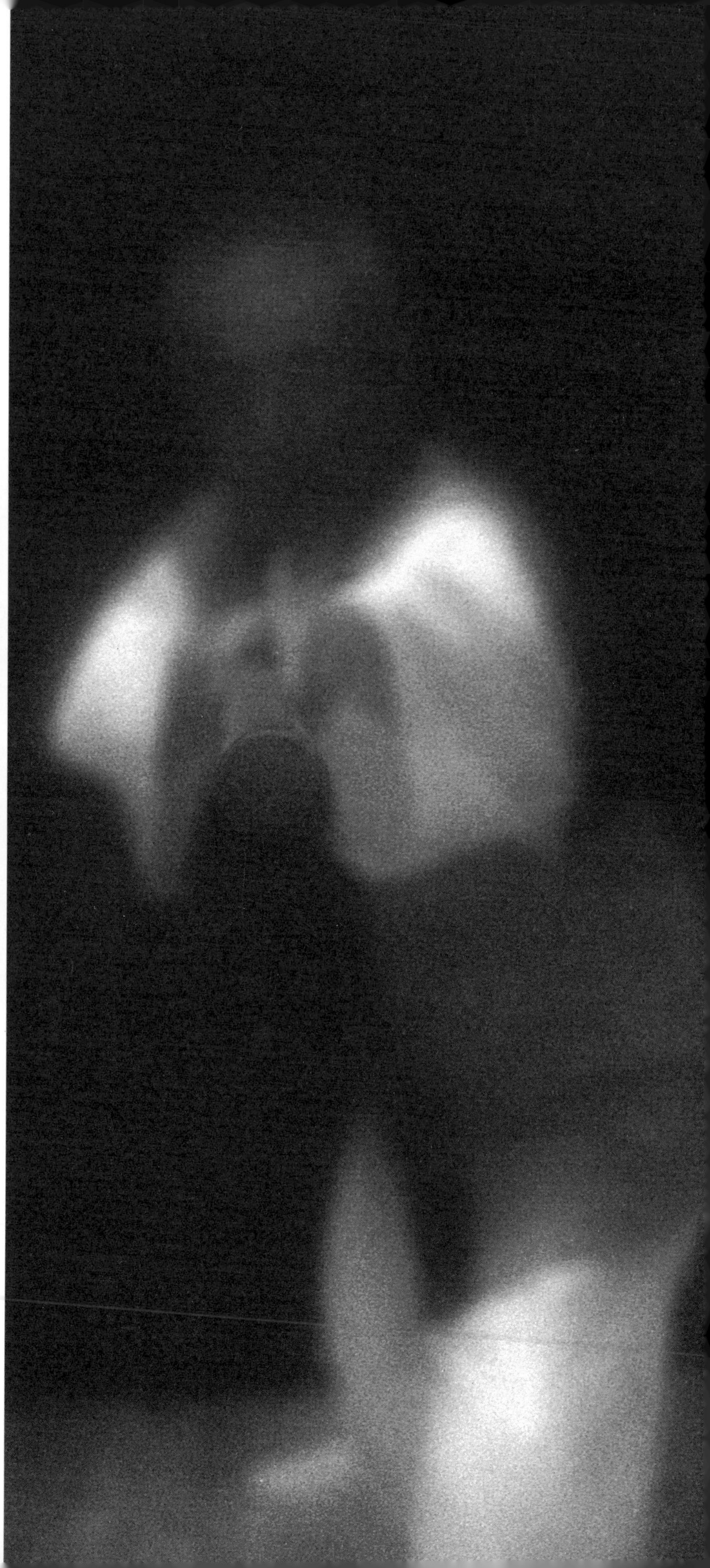

Keiko Sabaki Kata

Methods of Training in stick fighting

When training with the stick it is important to practice correct form. However, before this, it is necessary to train in Jūtai-jutsu. Within stick fighting, thrusting techniques are often held to be important. In a verse of the gokui: "striking the void, if there is a response in your hands, that is the gokui." You must have the enlightenment of the Buddha of the void (kokū-bosatsu), whose heart was as infinite as the void itself. Thrusting the bō into the mist is in truth thrusting one's heart and mind, and this is one method of kokū—void training. In order to obtain the correct type of thrust, practice by driving a 5-sun nail into a wooden pillar, thrusting at the head of the nail with the bō. At first, the nail will often fly out, but this is to be expected. Once you have mastered this technique using just the stick and arms, the next step is to strike and pull back with the entire body. When doing this, do not hold the stick with strength, instead allow the stick to dance in the space. Rather than striking out and pulling back, let it float. Your body should also assume a lightness as if floating, while maintaining balance.

If your bō is struck up by the opponent's sword, it is important not to resist the blow, rather you should harmonize with the motion. Then, use kyō-jutsu (present truth) to discern the hidden aim of the opponent and strike them before they can execute the move. Attacking the opponent before their own attack has formed; this is the art of seizing the flower before it blooms (debana). The expression "debana" can be traced to the *Fushikaden* ("Flower of Appearance," a Noh drama book of the 15th century). It refers to the state of a flower just before blossoming. It is essential to grasp a vision of the miraculous truth of tai-jutsu, in which the stick and body are one in the mist.

GOKYŌ GOKAI IHEN SABAKI GATA
五境五界謂変捌型

This changes into the 25 techniques of Kasumi no Hō. Further, by combining the ura and omote, this becomes 50 techniques.

Gohō 五法

Hira Ichimonji no Kamae. 1. Spin the bō to the right and left. 2. Strike the opponent's left leg with the right end of the bō. 3. Strike to the left side of the opponent's head with the right end of the bō. 4. Strike the opponent's right leg with the end of the bō. 5. Rotating the bō overhead, strike the opponent's right leg.

Ura Gohō 裏五法

Hira Ichimonji. 1. Spin the bō to the left and right. 2. Pull the right foot back and thrust. 3. Strike the left side of the head with the end of the bō. 4. Strike up into the opponent's leg with the right end of the bō. 5. Releasing the left hand, turn the bō and strike to the left side of the opponent's head.

Sashiai 差合

Chūdan no Kamae. 1. Thrust. 2. Slide the bō back and strike the opponent's left side with the tail of the bō. 3. Rotate the left end of the bō and strike up with a gedan strike.

Funabari 船張

Gedan no Kamae. 1. Strike the opponent's left side with the right end of the bō. 2. Strike the opponent's head with the tail of the bō. 3. Pulling the right foot back, strike up with the right end of the bō. 4. Strike down to the top of the opponent's head with end of the bō.

Tsuru no Issoku 鶴の一足

Ten Chi Jin no Kamae. 1. Slam the bō down onto the opponent's foot. 2. Strike into both legs from the left side with the end of the bō. 3. Strike to the right side of the opponent's head with the end of the bō. 4. Strike the crown of the head with the end of the bō. 5. Strike the left side of the opponent's head with the end of the bō. 6. Release your left hand and strike the opponent's left leg with the left end of the bō.

Ri Iissoku 裏一足

Gedan no Kamae. 1. Strike the left leg of the opponent's clothing. 2. Strike to the right leg 3. Hurl the bō over with the left hand, and strike the opponent's head. 4. Strike the crown of the head with the end of the bō. 5. Strike the left-hand side of the opponent's head with the bō. 6. Releasing the left hand, strike the opponent's left leg with the left end of the bō. 7. Thrust.

Suso Otoshi 裾落

Chūdan no Kamae. 1. Thrust with the bō. 2. Release the left hand and strike the opponent's left side. 3. From that position strike the right leg with the left end of the bō. 4. Hurl the bō up and over with the right hand, and strike the opponent's crown. 5. Strike up with the left end of the bō to the opponent's left leg.

Ura Suso Otoshi 裏裾落

Chūdan no Kamae. 1. Thrust. 2. Strike to the opponent's left leg 3. Strike to the opponent's right leg. 4. Strike to the opponent's left leg. 5. Strike to the opponent's right leg. 6. Throw the right end of the bō over, and strike the opponent's head. 7. Thrust.

Ippon Sugi 一本杉

Tenchijin no Kamae. 1. Slam the bō down onto the opponent's foot. 2. Stepping back, strike the opponent's left leg with the end of the bō. 3. Throw the left-hand end of the bō over and, turning, strike the opponent's right side. 4. From this position strike to the crown of the opponent's head with the end of the bō. 5. Step back and, hurling the right end of the bō over, strike to the opponent's crown.

Taki Otoshi 瀧落

Chūdan no Kamae. 1. Thrust with the bō 2. With the left hand, turn the bō behind your back to come out over your shoulder and strike the left side of the opponent's head. 3. Rotating your right hand and putting the bō under your right arm, turn the bō behind your back to come out over your left shoulder, and strike the right side of the opponent's head. 4. Releasing the left hand, strike to the right, then strike to the left side of the opponent's head.

Kokū 虚空

Thrust from Chūdan no Kamae. Strike up the opponent's blow coming in to the left from the right, then jump in and strike to the head. 1. Stepping back with the right leg, bend the right arm and raise the left arm up to receive the strike. 2. Taking a big step back with the left leg and rotating the left end of the bō over, strike to the opponent's left side. 3. From this position strike the left leg.

Kasa no Uchi 笠之内

Seigan no Kamae. 1. From this position strike the opponent's right side. 2. Pulling the left leg back, strike the opponent's left side. 3. Strike up from below with the end of the bō.

Tachi Otoshi 太刀落

Ichimonji no Kamae. 1. The opponent cuts in. 2. Bending the left arm, raise the right arm high to receive the strike. 3. From this position, step back with your left foot. At the same time strike down to the opponent's wrist from above with the right end of the stick. 4. Releasing the left end of the bō, strike the opponent's head with the left hand.

Harai 払

Ichimonji no Kamae. 1. The opponent cuts in. 2. Stepping back with the left leg, strike down on the opponent's right wrist from above with the right end of the bō. 3. Strike upwards to the opponent's wrist with the left end of the bō.

Kote Tsuki 小手附

Chūdan no Kamae. 1. Thrust out. 2. Pulling the bō back, strike to the opponent's left side. 3. Flip the left end of the stick and strike down to the opponent's head. 4. Turn the bō and strike to the wrists.

Mukōzume 向詰

Ihen no Kamae (or Hokoya no Kamae). Flipping the bō, strike with the right end of the bō down to the opponent's head. Repeat three times.

Keriage 蹴り挙げ

Ihen no Kamae. Flip the right end of the bō to strike down to the opponent's head. Repeat five times. On the fifth time, release the left hand and strike up as though kicking. Strike in to the left side of the opponent.

Gekiryū 撃留

Left Seigan no Kamae. 1. Thrust. 2. Strike to the side of the opponent's head with the end of the bō. 3. Stepping back with the left leg, thrust left with the end of the bō. 4. Rotate the end of the stick and strike the opponent's left side.

Tsukeiri 附入

Right Seigan no Kamae. 1. Left thrust. 2. Strike the opponent's side with the end of the bō. 3. Flip the end of the bō and thrust. This is also known as Wangetsu no Kamae.

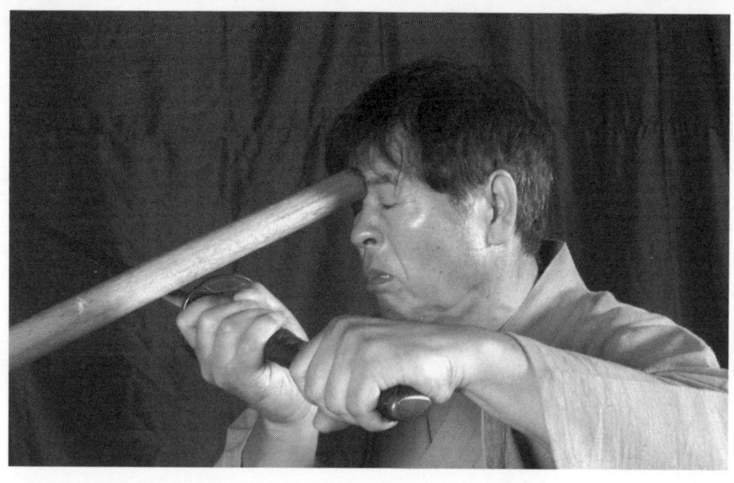

Gorin Kudaki 五輪砕

Left Ihen no Kamae (this is also known as Jocho no Kamae—"riding on a snake"). The kyūsho known as "Gorin" means to point at "chi-sui-ka-fu-ku." 1. Spinning the bō, strike the opponent's left side. 2. Spin the bō and strike to the opponent's right side. 3. Repeat this three times.

Tenchijin 天地人

Tenchijin no Kamae. 1. Rotate the bō to the left and strike up from gedan. 2. Change to a thrust. 3. From this position strike to the right side of the opponent's head with the end of the bō. 4. From there step forward with the right foot and strike the opponent's left leg. 5. Step back with the right leg and thrust.

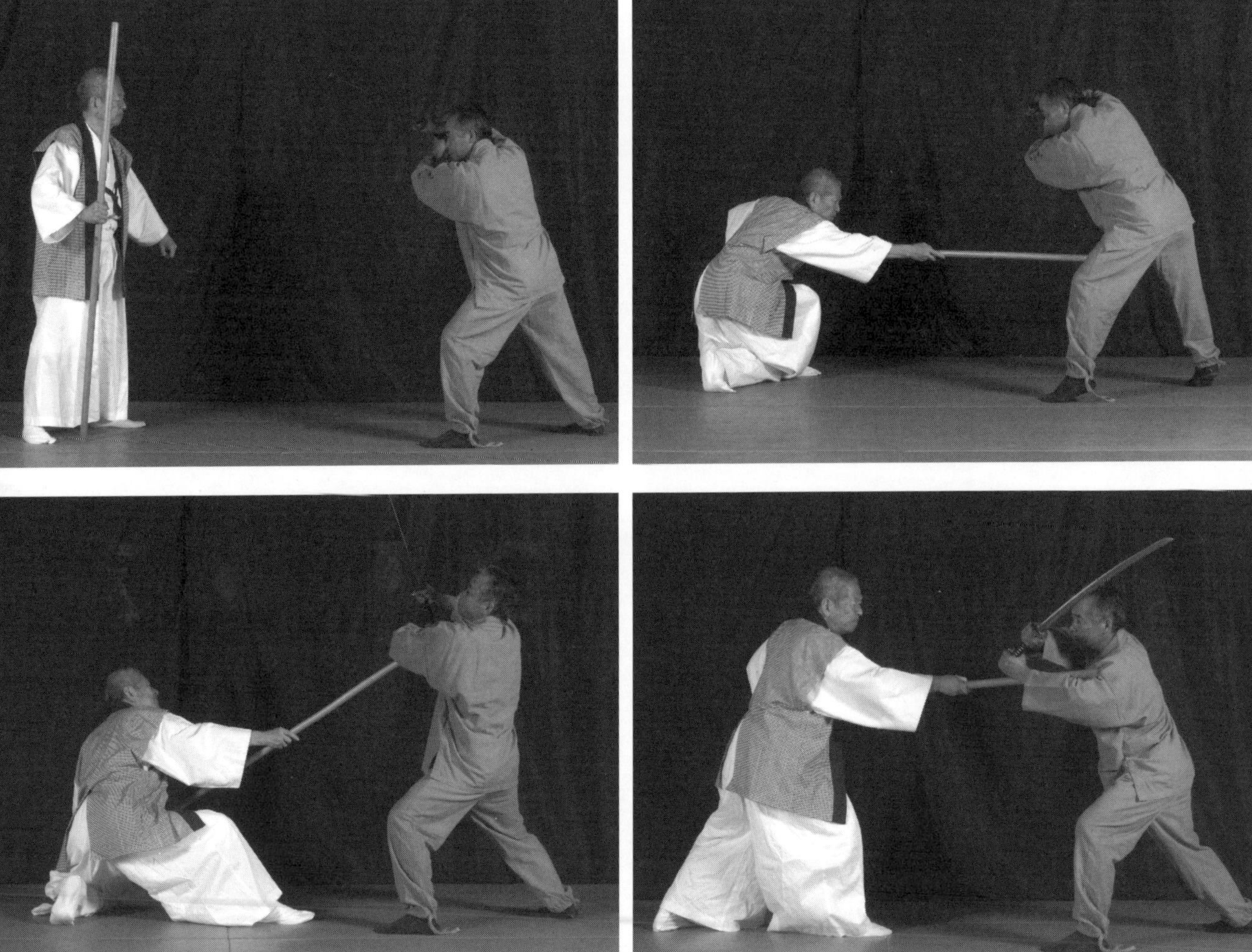

Maehiro 前広

Chūdan no Kamae. 1. Enter striking to the opponent's left side. 2. Strike. the opponent's head with the end of the stick. 3. Leap back one step and, as in Ipponsugi, slam the stick down. 4. Thrust with the right leg on the floor.

Ryō Kote 両小手

Chūdan no Kamae. 1. Step back and strike up with the end of the bō hitting both wrists of the opponent. 2. Strike the opponent's head with the end of the stick. 3. From this position strike up from gedan with the end of the stick. 4. From there strike the opponent's left leg with the end of the stick.

Uranami 浦波

Ihen no Kamae. 1. Strike out and pull back with the bō. 2. Flip the end of the bō and strike the opponent's head. 3. Pull the bō back, thrust. 4. Release the right hand and rotate the bō behind your back under your left arm, and strike the opponent's left side.

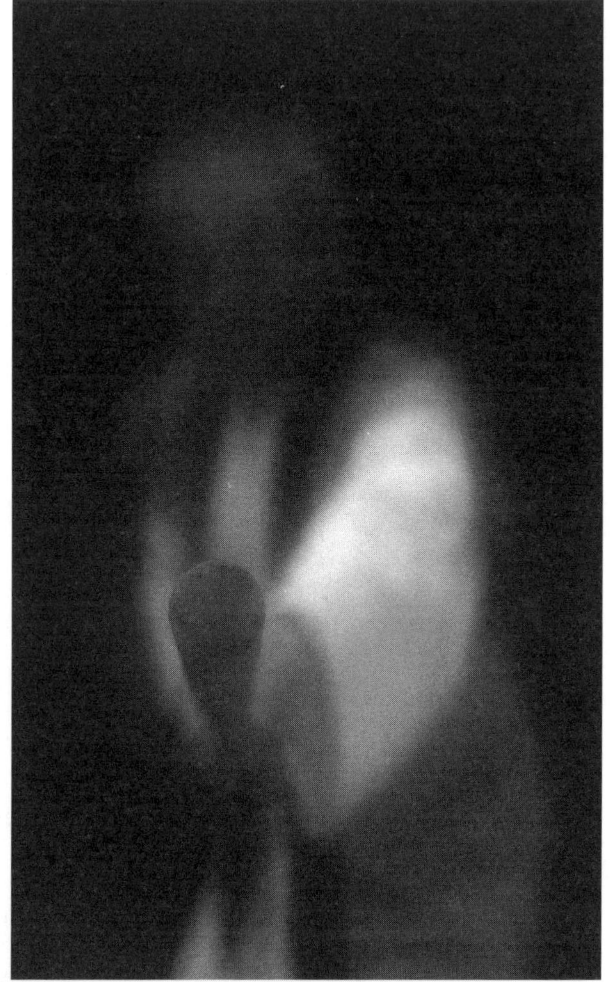

Tama Gaeshi 玉返

Ihen no Kamae. 1. Thrust at the opponent's head. 2. Pull back and strike the opponent's left side with the end of the bō. 3. Flip the bō with the left hand and thrust into the left side of the opponent's head. 4. From this position strike the opponent's left leg. 5. From there strike gedan with the left end of the bō.

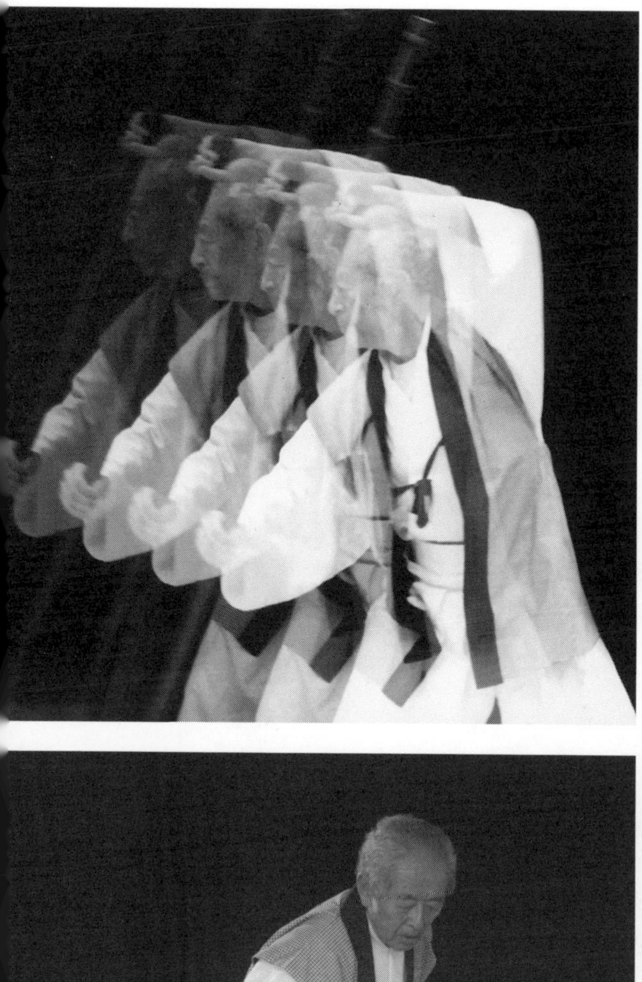

Jō-jutsu

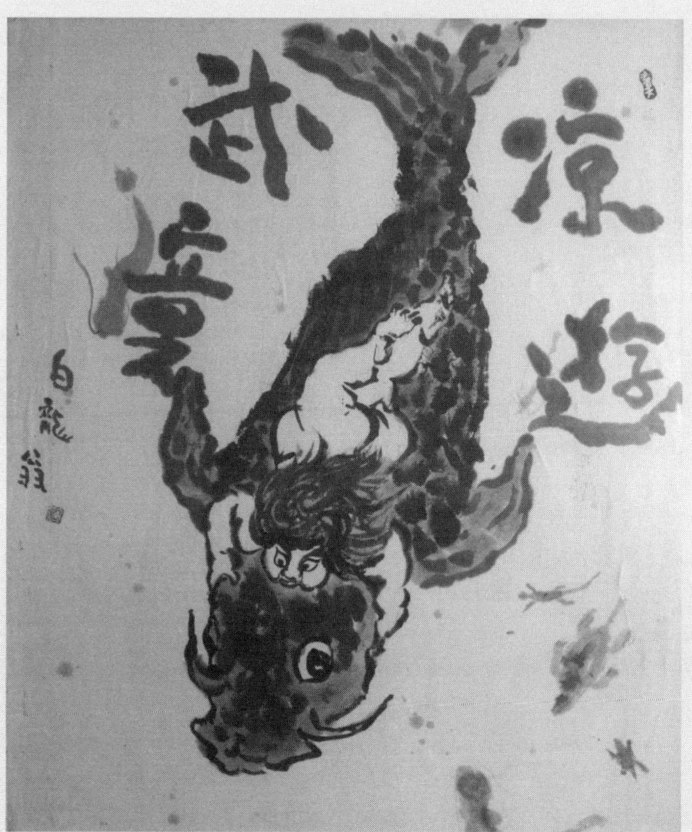

Ryōyū Budō

Author with the Zulus. He was given the name of "Hillock"

Sticks are not just about wood

The essence of bō-jutsu is also the essence of life. One ordinary stick can be used for many things. For example, when entering enemy territory, walking stealthily carrying a stick in one hand will indicate to the opponent that you have come to attack. However, if you were to disguise the same stick and walk dragging one leg, the opponent would be caught off their guard. These kinds of tactics, adjusted according to the situation, show how effective a slight change in your thinking can be to enhance the use of the bō. This bō-jutsu is known as the "deceptive or changing bō" (ihen no bō; see page 68).

There are various ways to instill fear into an opponent. If the opponent shows fear of your weapon, you can exploit this fear by spinning the stick. You must strike at the areas that your opponent finds mentally painful (itai)—this is also an aspect of mastering stick fighting. It is possible to transpose the sound of the word "painful" (itai, 痛い) onto another reading: 意多意 (itai), meaning "thinking many thoughts;" or one might say where the opponent's consciousness/intent is focused, which translates as "plural consciousness," "multiple thoughts." Thus, the pain one inflicts can be understood to be both physical and psychological.

Those who think that the bō is all thrusting, striking, and spinning show a considerable lack of experience in their ability to read and plan tactics. In today's difficult times, I admire people who are honest and consistent, like a straight bō, and I would like to emphasize that one should live like this. However, it is doubtful your opponent will be honest with you. You must be mindful of how your opponent will use his weapon. Let's say your opponent draws the stick back for some reason. You may think that they have lost their hostile intent towards you. Yet that instant will create a big opening, and your opponent's stick may strike you. This kind of deception will be to the opponent's advantage, proving they have outwitted you. Even if someone appears unintelligent and with no social standing, if they are consistent and persevere, they have the potential to one day become great. If you are able to fully master an ordinary stick through training, then even as an ordinary person you can become extraordinary. This is one of the esteemed qualities of Bō-jutsu.

The quintessence of budō is something that cannot be seen. Simply put, if you develop yourself by training tirelessly using a simple bō, you will manifest the world of "ultra-consciousness," purify your heart, and gain the calmness of

Dressed as a Shugendō Priest holding a Butoku-jō.

a fresh spirit—then you will know peace of mind. Furthermore, you will gain self-confidence and dispel all manner of fears. This is because the essence of budō is within bō-jutsu. The Swiss psychoanalyst and theologian, Dr. Paul Tournier (1898–1986) said, "aggression is similar to Freud's libido as a manifestation of human life force and, in this sense, is something that lurks in every person." Furthermore, Raymond A. Dart also stated that there is only one reason that human beings were able to break loose from their anthropoid ancestors; namely that they were expert killers. In these statements the relationship between the violence that lurks within humankind and weapons is very clear.

It is said that the history of humankind goes back five to six million years. Borrowing the phrase from Dart, in the long history of natural selection (touta), or many fights (touta), we have survived because of our killer instinct. If this is the case, mankind today, by learning bō-jutsu, the path to the world of super consciousness, must strive to change the world from one of war and massacre into a true and great world of peace.

Jūmonji 十文字

Ihen no Kamae. 1. Thrust to the face. 2. Pull back and strike the opponent's left side with the end of the jō. 3. Flip the left hand and thrust to the opponent's face. 4. From this position, strike the opponents left leg. 5. From here strike gedan with the left end of the jō.

Roppō 六法

Gedan no Kamae. 1. From this position turn the body and strike the opponent's left leg, releasing the right hand, and turn the bō onto the shoulder and strike the left side of the opponent's head. 3. Rotate the left hand and thrust.

Kyūho 九法

Chūdan no Kamae. 1. Strike up to gedan from the lower right. 2. Pulling the left leg back, strike the left side of the opponent's head with the right end of the jō. 3. Strike the opponent's head with the left end of the jō. 4. From this position strike gedan. 5. Strike the opponent's left leg with the right end of the jō. 6. Turning the right hand over, thrust.

Hiryū 飛龍

Tenchijin no Kamae. 1. Strike the opponent's shoulder with the jō. 2. Strike the opponent's head with the end of the jō. 3. Turning the right hand, strike the opponent's head again. 4. Pull the left leg back and strike the opponent's side. 5. Step in with the left leg and strike up to gedan with the end of the jō. 6. Pull the left leg back and strike to the side of the opponent's head. 7. Strike the opponent's leg with the left end of the jō. 8. Pull the left leg back and strike into the opponent's left side.

飛龍
構
二
三
四
五
六
七
八
九

Tsukeiri 附入

Chūdan no Kamae. 1. Stepping back with the right leg, strike the opponent's left temple (kasumi) with the left end of the stick. 2. Releasing the left hand, strike the left temple. 3. Repeat three times and finish with a strike to the head.

附入

Udekake 腕掛

Ichimonji no Kamae. 1. The opponent cuts in with a Tachi. 2. Step back with the left leg, with the right hand up and the left hand down. 3. Release the left hand and strike into the arm.

Kote Gaeshi 小手返

Seigan no Kamae. 1. The attacker thrusts out, but this is meant to trick the opponent. 2. In fact, as he does this, he rotates the hand and strikes the opponent's side. There are ten contact points on the opponent's body. The attacker has thirty-six forms of attack. Thirty-six is divisible by nine, which is a number with deep religious and philosophical meanings.

太刀落

Tachi Otoshi 太刀落

Seigan no Kamae. 1. As you strike at your opponent's head, your opponent will also attempt to strike your head. 2. Pulling the left hand back, strike kote. 3. Keeping your left knee on the ground, strike up to kote from below.

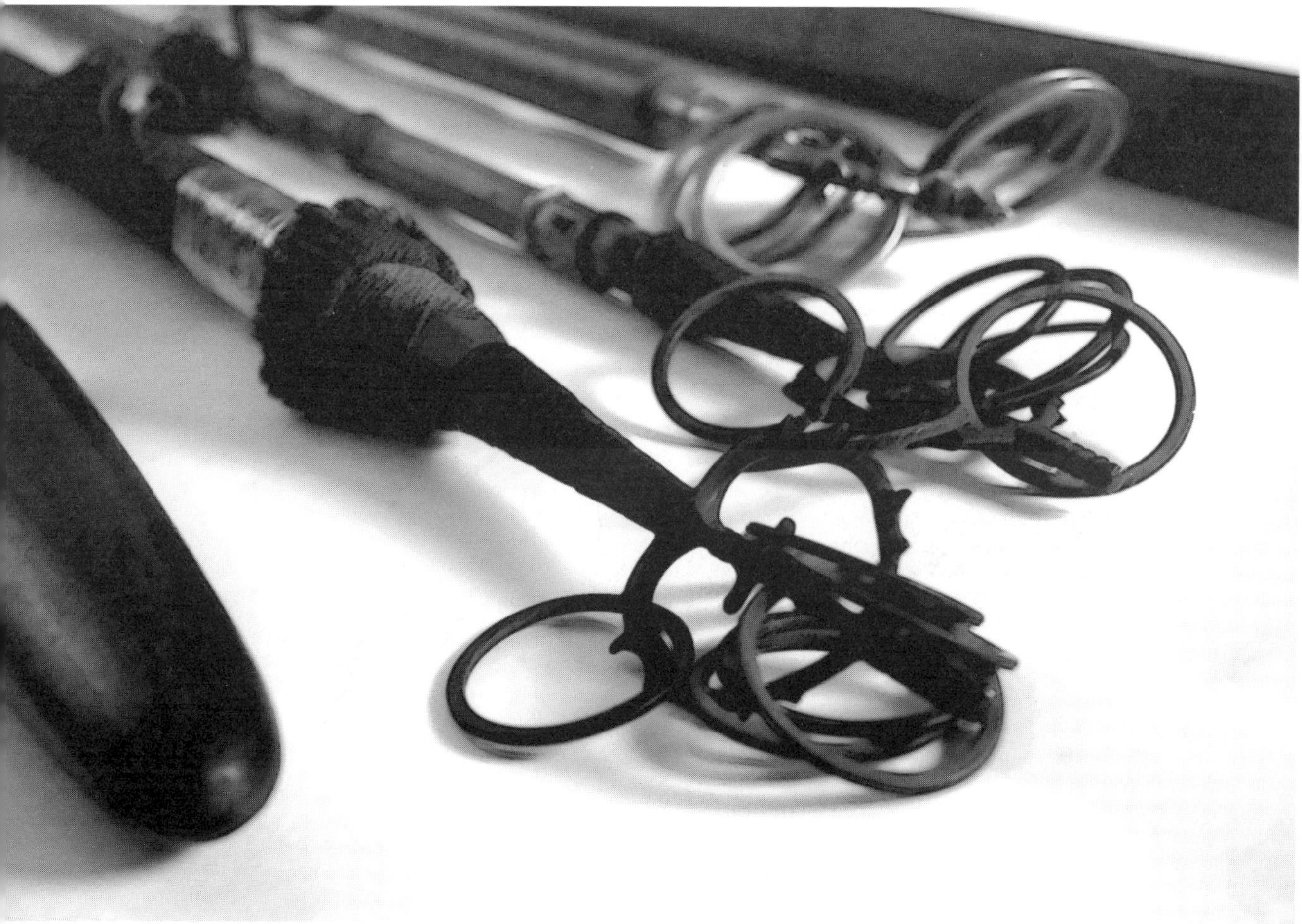

Bō Nuke

Marishiten (God of War)

Kubi Nuke I　首抜けI

首抜け

Kubi Nuke II　首抜けII

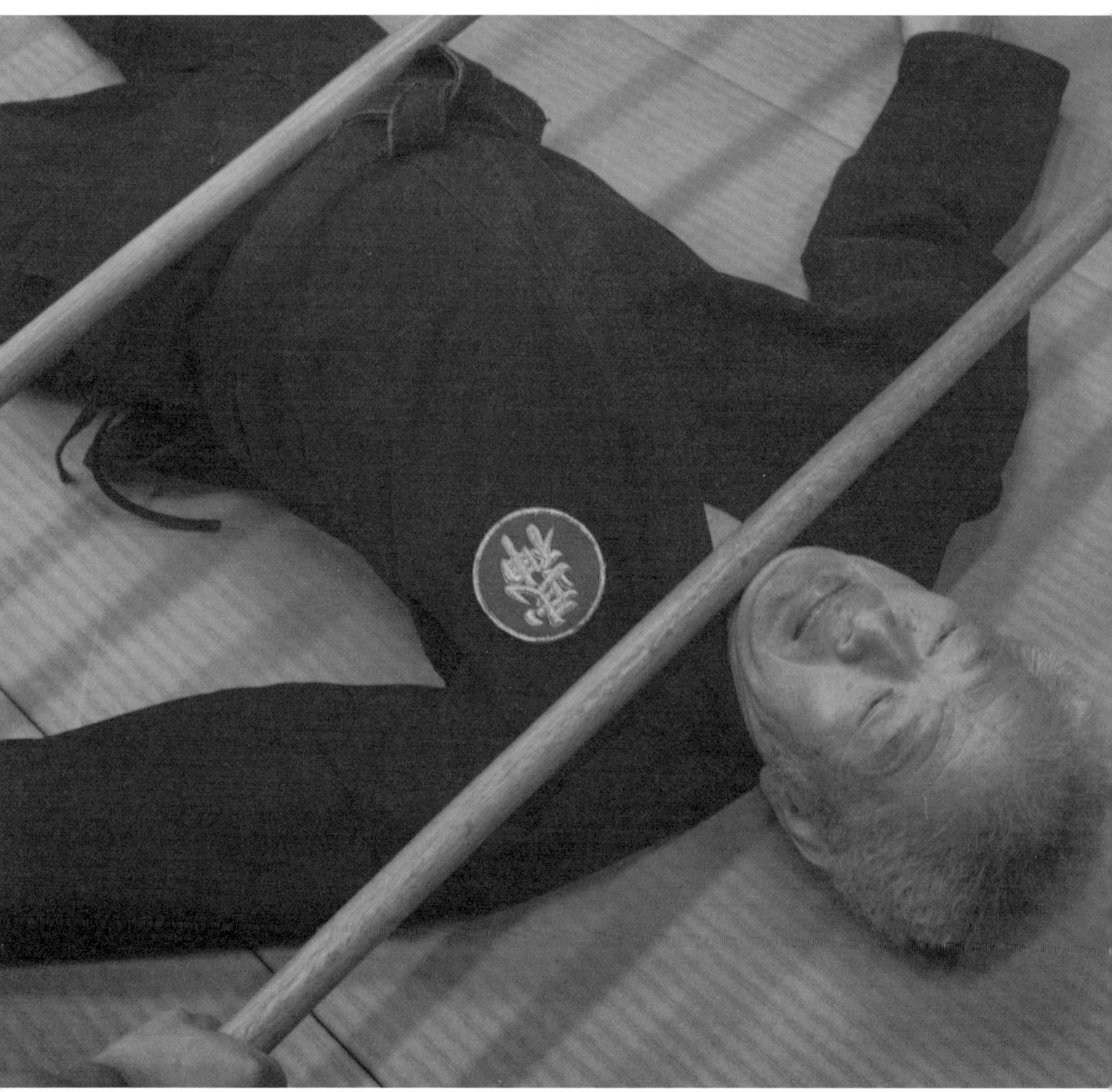

投げ棒

Nage Bō 投げ棒

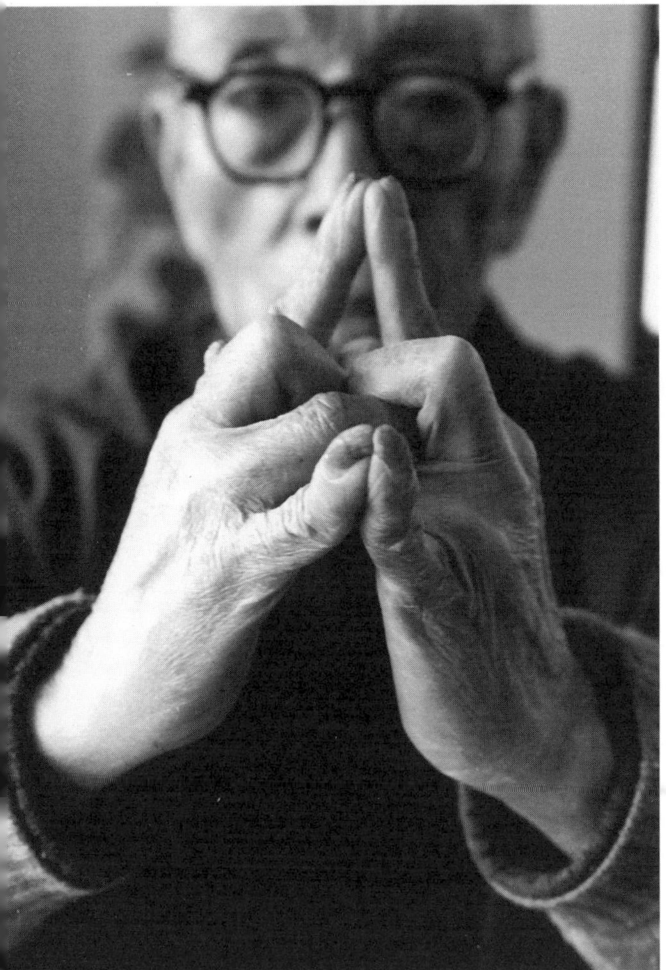

Bō-jutsu of Takamatsu Toshitsugu Sensei

The monument to Takamatsu Toshitsugu sensei, built on the thirty-third anniversary of his death

A demonstration of bō-jutsu by Takamatsu sensei (left)

Takamatsu sensei teaching bō-jutsu at a university

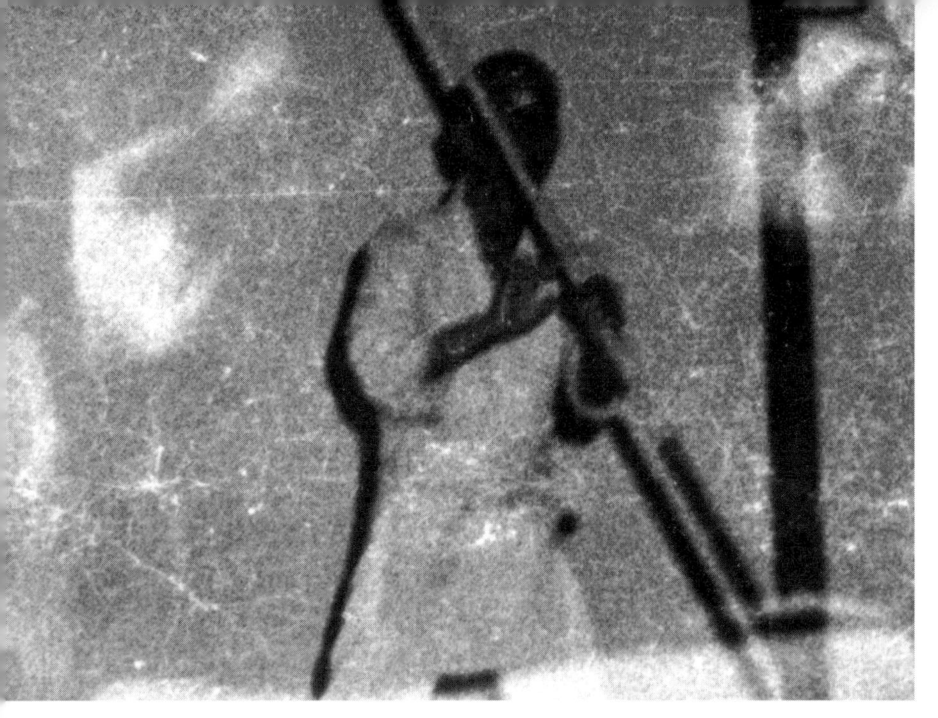
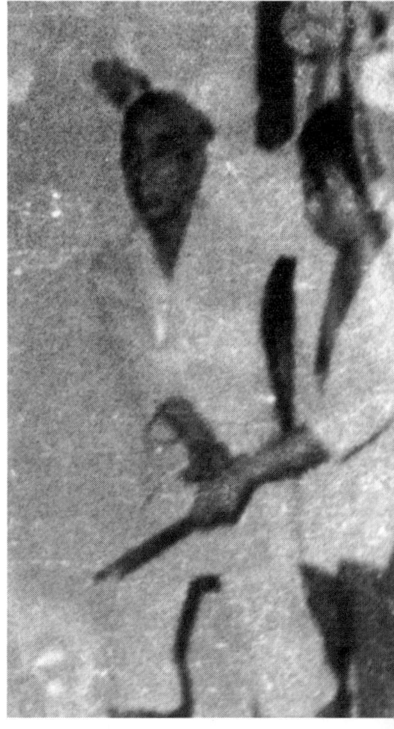

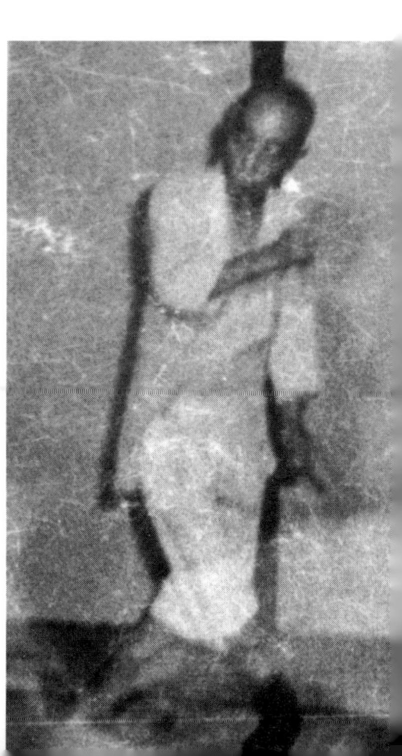

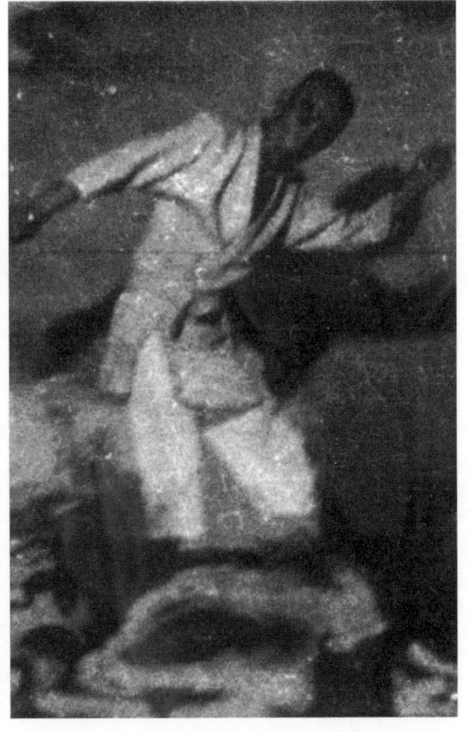

From Left: Daikokuten (God of Wealth); Benzaiten (Goddess of Music, Fine Arts, Eloquence, Literature); Bishamonten (God of Dignity and the Harbinger of Good Fortune)

A painting by Takamatsu Toshitsugu sensei

Shinobi-zue

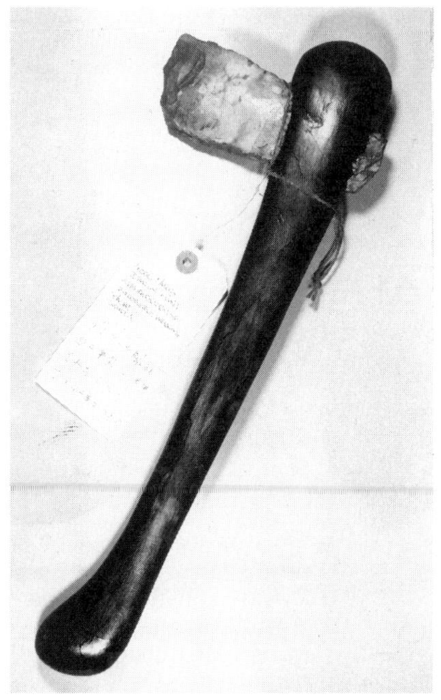

Stone Axe

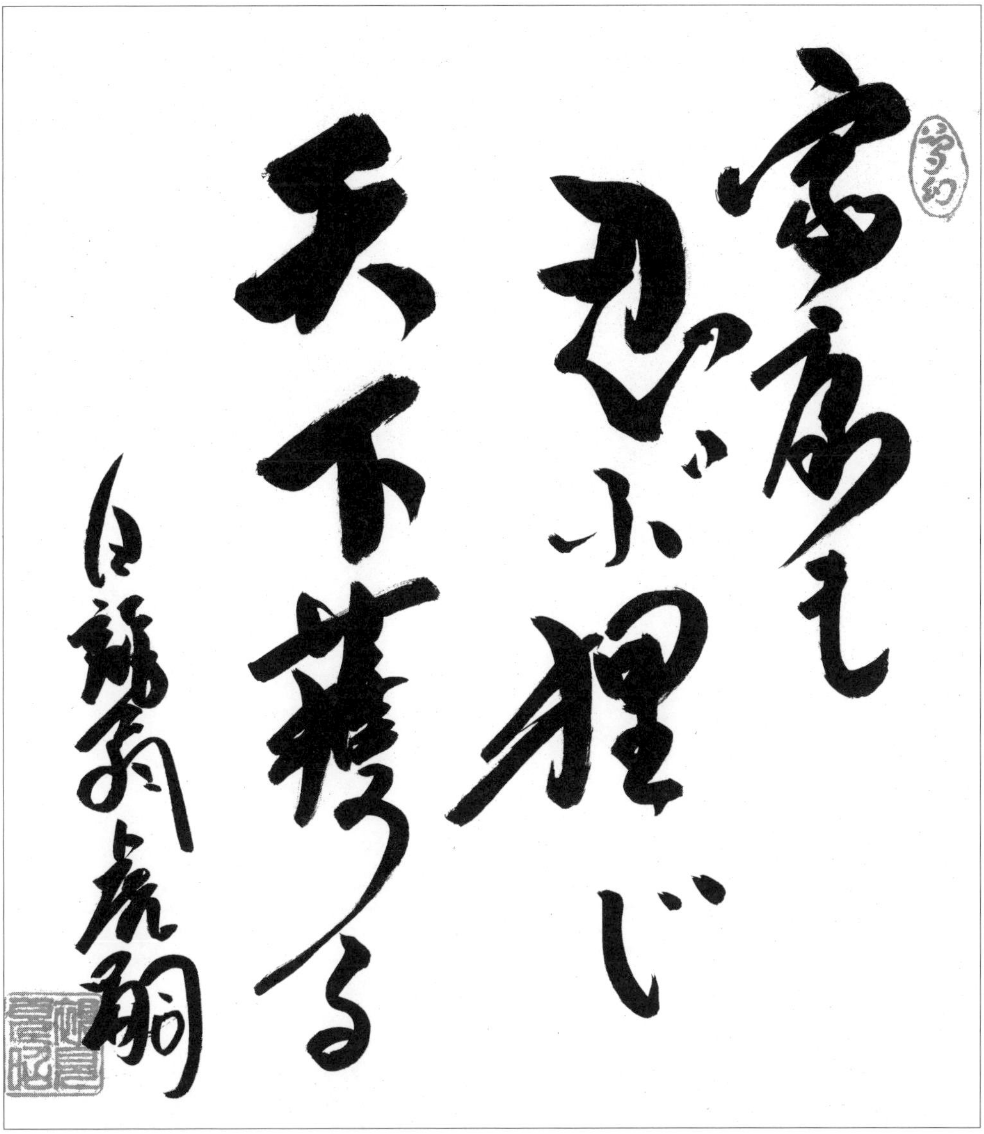

家康も
忍ぶ狸じ
天下獲る

After great perseverance, Ieyasu ruled supreme over Japan (by the author)

The nickname of Shōgun Tokugawa Ieyasu was "Racoon dog"

Falling water soon begins its ascent

Izumo Takeru no Bō

MAIN TEXT

「武士道」という言葉を使う前に

「武士道」という言葉がある。字義通りに言えば「武士の道」だ。武士として高い地位を得た、ということでは、その先駆けとなったのが平清盛(1118-1181)である。それまでの武士たち、すなわち侍は文字通り「さぶらう者」(さむらい)であって、特別の場合を除いて昇殿も許されなかった。清盛が武将でありながら太政大臣にまで登りつめ、国政に関与することができたというのは、やはり武士、侍としての多角的な感覚を持っていたからに違いない。一芸は万芸に通ずる。たとえば彼は優れた兵法家であり、軍隊を集めるのも、またそれを率いて戦うのも上手だった。それと同時に政治力も備え、さらに多くの部下を養うだけの経済力もあった。政治力というのはけっして駆け引きばかりではなくて、大事なのは時代の先を読むことである。その後の織田信長(1534-1582)にしろ、徳川家康(1542-1616)にしろ、天下をとった人間はひとしく時代の先を見抜く先見力があった。

了知する感覚(勘覚と言いたい)こそが武道の極意の第一ポイントである。それは聖人のように、未来を予言するような位にあることを意味する。

戦いの本質も、同じく、先を予知することである。武道において、予知する動物のシンボルとされているのが虎である。虎とは事象と物と人について、予知、察知、そして看破することを意味している。先を予知して、勝敗のこだわりから離れて生き抜くこと。このことは、戦いと競争にさいなまれている今の時代にはますます重要になっていると私は思う。しかも大事なのは、知覚的物理的に予知するのでなくて、潜在意識から超意識でもって予知、察知し、気配に応じて自らが動いていくことである。(もっとも、ただじっと座って静観しているほうが良い場合もある)。ただし、そういう超感覚の状態に入れる人というのは、じつに少ない。

一般的には、そういう限られた人のことを天才と呼ぶのだろうが、天才というのはつまるところ、人間以外のものに変われる才能になってくる。それは文字通りの「天の才能」ではなくて、「転ずる才能」。必要に応じて自在に、例えば虫にも獣にも転化できる「転才」である。虫や獣そして植物には予知する能力がある。その予知感覚を彼らと共有してこそ、神仏の意識につながる。自然力、転生はそこから生まれる。すなわち転才とは、自然意識というか超感覚が人間よりすごい優れもののことであり、兵法家として求めるところは、その転才を養うことにある。このことを天地人三才の法と言う。

そうした能力を修行とか稽古によって、ある程度は養うことはできる。とはいえ、たとえ長年稽古を続けていても、できるようになる人とできない人がいるものだ。しかし、超感覚がそれなりにあったとしても、平清盛のように宿敵の武将の二人の幼児(後の源頼朝と義経)の助命を嘆願され、聞き入れてしまうような優しさがあると、没後、成人したその二人の手で一族を根絶やしにされてしまう憂き目にあう。まさに「平家物語」に記されているごとく、「諸行無常の響きあり」だ。武士道の徳目には仁義礼智信があり、それら五常は仁から始まるという。五常は五情とも言って、武士の情の要素がある。だが、やはりそうした心の優しさや、人の良さ、言い換えれば心に巣くう甘さを厳しく排し、自己を律することのできた武士のみが、結局は乱

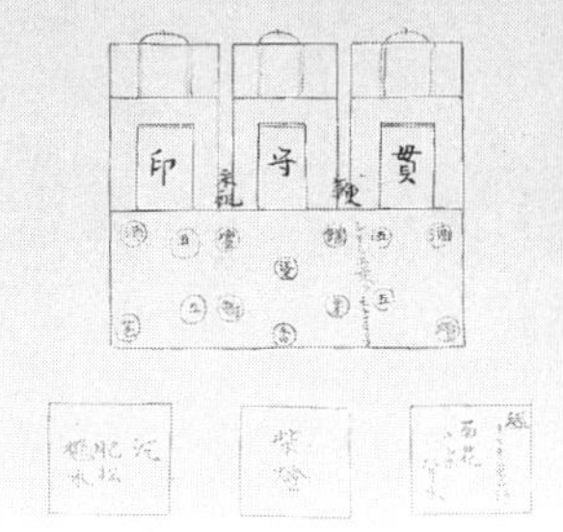

の中を生き延び、名を成している。そうでないと強運を呼び込めないのだろうか。とはいえ、これには時の流れという一面もあるのだが。

この超感覚とは「兆感覚」でもある。「兆」に「しんにょう」を添えると「逃」(逃げる、避けるの意)になる。忍術とは護る、避ける、逃げるための大事な感覚であることを、この文字は表しているのである。

もっとも、仁薄き武将は、信望は集めにくい。源頼朝は自分に心から従おうとはしない、弟の義経の命を奪った。後世の人気がないゆえんである。徳川家康は主君の織田信長に命じられて、無念にも長男の信康を切腹させた。そうした、いわば踏み絵を踏むような辛棒辛棒が、後の徳川三百年の基礎を作り、神君家康と謳われるに至った。「堪忍は無事長久の基、怒りは敵と思え」とは家康の言葉である。にもかかわらず、家康が、「狸親父」と蔑まれる原因のひとつがそこにある。

「自然体」を知れ

現代人は、「武士道」というと大道寺友山(1639-1730)の「武道初心集」とか、山本常朝(1659-1719)の「葉隠」とか剣豪・宮本武蔵(1584-1645)の「五輪書」を読んだり、あるいはそれらについての参考文献を見て、武士道は素晴らしいものと思いこんでいる。

たしかに、「武士道とは死ぬことと見つけたり」(「葉隠」)、「我事(わがごと)において後悔をせず」(宮本武蔵「独行道」)といった言葉に見るごとく、そうした名著に記された武士道は素晴らしいものだ。しかし私は、それらの書物はあくまでも彼らの随筆であり、彼らの「徒然草」だと思う。残念ながら、武蔵も含めて、彼らの実体験というのは行き着くところまでは行き着いていない。武道の極意には到達していない。彼らの体験したもの、書いてあることは、まさに幻影だ。有名なフランス映画、ジャン・ルノワール監督の「大いなる幻影」と変わらない。オット・プレミンジャーの「愚かな妻」となる。

ここで肝に銘じてほしいのは、極意とは頂点ではないということだ。それは平坦なものである。そう、極意とは「平常心」であり、自然力であり、だからこそ「武風一貫」という言葉があるのだ。「極意を求めるような感覚でいつまでもいると、極意の本質を失ってしまう」と私は常々言っている。

今の武士道のブームなるものは、幻影の世界を求めているだけのもの。騎士道なき今、武道家も含めて多くの人が、武士道の幻を求めてドン・キホーテのドラマを自ら演じているようなものだ。ただし、そこから本物の武道、不滅の価値観の宿っている武士道に惹かれていく人も出てくる。

武道には表技と裏技がある。その表裏一体の妙というよりも、その虚と実の間にある転換(というより「天勘」である)の妙を知らなければならない。幻覚であるという妙実(たいじつ、すなわち体術)も妙の一つである。

じつは武士道のひとつとして大切なのは「自然力」(自然妙)ということだ。わが師・高松寿嗣先生のように、生活人として淡々と毎日を送りつつも、超感覚を身につけ、いわゆる剣豪をもしのぐ修羅場をたびたびくぐり抜けてきた人物がいる。たしかに武人として国に仕えたり主君

米麥粟 小豆
大豆 松緑
蓬 菖蒲 菊花
沉 肥松 榧木
餅土 鹽海 栗山 鮒川
潮
北斗水
第一願主浄衣
第二七度禮拝
第三水印結曰誦文
第四護身法
第五九字
第六六根清浄祓
第七守尊之誦文
第八正命之誦文
第九拝眞之團ヲ取三度
第十供奠之鞭取テ
第十一祈現之扇取三度
第十二柴燈ヲタキツケ禮讃之圖
第十三守尊之誦文
ヲ唱テ祈也
敬禮退下〻〻〻
第十四當流祖彌拝禮
東方構寶廟奉懸守印

に仕えたり理想に殉じたりすることは大事である。だが、それを超越することこそが、国を守ることであり、主君を守ることであり、理想を貫くことだと私は思う。それこそがほんとうの武士であり、そこに流れるものこそ武士道なのだ。

陰に徹することのできる人ならば、己を無にして陰に徹し善を求めることだ。そして淡々として生きる。武道家も、政治家も、その陰を求め、さまざまな形で陰を慕うものだ。たとえば徳川家康は天海僧正(1536–1643)という、陰の僧侶に智恵を仰いでいた。天海は裏から家康を動かし、「黒衣の宰相」と陰で呼ばれていたのである。日本の歌謡曲の作曲家の大御所として知られる古賀政男(1904–78)の作品に「影を慕いて」がある。日本の心を謳った名曲として名高いのも不思議ではない。

「三尺下がって師の影を踏まず」というのが師に対する礼節とされるが、闘うとき影を前方に落として、敵に対して自分の影を盾とする位取り、すなわち陽光に隠れる位取りこそが武道の陰である。忍術では「遁影」という言葉がある。影を前方の盾とする「盾の影」のことである。

世の中には見かけ倒しの、表面を飾っただけの人やものがあまりにも多く、裏社会の方がなにかを動かす大きな力があるのはご存じの通り。氷山にしても、下が重いから海中に浮かんでいる。仮に、表からは窺えない海中に沈んでいる膨大な氷の部分がないとしたら、人が飛びつこうとしても飛びつけない。氷山もろとも、あっという間に沈んでしまうことだろう。

私は最近、本当の伝統ある武士道、すなわち幻影でない武士道というものが、真剣に求められるようになってきたと実感している。

先人たちが命を賭けて代々伝え守ってきた本当の武士道というのは、思想であり哲学であり、宗教であり、生き方の基本であり、生活の知恵であり、はたまた武道のテクニックでもある。それは素晴らしいことであると同時に、そうした人間生活全般に活用されるべき本当の武士道を行じていかない限り、けっして生きていけない、そして自分を護ることはできない、ということを読者はぜひ、この本から学び取ってほしい。本当の武士道を貫き、自分自身をコントロールしなければいけないのだ。

これが武者修業だ

国際テロ、地球温暖化、環境破壊などの諸問題を見据え、世界武者修行の終局として2003年夏、アメリカのニュージャージーを訪問した。戻ってから血液検査をしたところ、320という異常に高い血糖値とAb-Alc9.2というヘモグロビンを見て、医者も仰天した。ところが一ヵ月後に検査したところ、今度は血糖値が160でヘモグロビンが7.1になっている。なぜか。それはいうまでもなく、すみやかに忍者生活に入り、肉類やアルコール分を摂取していた欧米型食事から忍者食に戻ったからだ。ご飯は玄米に小豆と黒豆と椎茸をいれて炊く。それに豆腐、ゴマ、味噌汁、無塩、無砂糖、火を通さざる物、色野菜という忍者食である。食事も満腹するほどまでは食べない。腹八分の基本八法に止める。満腹になると、精神も肉体も弛緩してしまい、急変に応じられなくなるからである。内臓も三回目の検査で今度は血糖値が130、ヘモグロビンが5.9になっていた。ほぼ2ヵ月でまったくの正常に返ったのである。とはいえ、73歳にして、老いは老いとしての悟りを大切にすることを、改めて思い知った次第である。

私は思う。戦いの期間のように、極限まで無理をして、死ぬ寸前にまで自分の心身を追いつめることもよい。昔ながらの過酷なまでの武道修業の目的はそうして内なる力を目覚めさせることにある。だが、しかるべき時期が来たら、するりと転じることだ。「転換」である。要は自己コントロールをすることだ。

山に籠ったり、世間から隔絶した生活をすることが武道の本来の修行ではない。自然体を保ち、自己をコントロールできるならば、修行の場は、あなたの、いま、そこにある。そして本当の武士道とは、けっしてそこから遠く離れたところにあるものではないのだ。師はよく言われた。「武道家でなくとも立派な人はようおりますからな……」と。

棒という武器

人類は武器といわれるものを、いつごろから使ったのであろうか。人類学者は、武器は木や石、さらには生物の骨の時代から始まって、銅の時代に至るといっている。また「人間は武器に先行したのではなく、武器が人間の進化をもたらした」とレイモンド・A・ダートはいう。また、ある歴史家によれば、人類の過去5000年の戦争の経過を探ってみると、戦争のなかった期間は5000年の中で280年にすぎなかったとのことだ。これは18日に一回しか平和な日がなかったという計算になる。武芸十八般というが、等しく18の数になるところが興味深い。

このように考えると、大多数の人が肯定している人間の進化進歩というものは非常に怖しいことになる。そこで、進化していない武器、棒の本質「棒術」を通して、人間の生きる方法を改めて見つめてみようと、私は声を大にして世界に気合いをいれはじめたのである。

棒術とは元来、自然のなかに発生したものだ。たとえばビーバーにしても、どこからか棒状のものをくわえてきて巣を作る。チンパンジーは器用に棒を使い食べものを取る。そこに棒術の萌芽がある。人類の旧石器時代はほぼ300万年前に始まるとされているが、当時から棒術はあった。鉄器や青銅器が生まれたことによって本当の武器が誕生したと思いこんでいる人も少なくないが、それ以前の時代から、とうに棒術が存在したということに思い至らないのはどうしたわけだろうか。

世界中に棒術があるが、風土や文化(とくに衣服)の関係で異なっているものだ。とくに日本は島国であり、江戸時代の鎖国政策もあって、歴史の中でさまざまに分化していった棒術を、秘密的に伝え守るという民族性があり、独自の棒術に発展していったのである。

棒術とは何か

客観写生を説いた俳人・高浜虚子(1874–1959)の俳句に「去年今年　貫く棒の如きもの」という作品がある。棒の魅力と神髄がここに描き出されている。

貫く棒といえば、私は高松寿嗣先生から「辛棒一貫」についての書をいただき、毎日、応接間に掲げられているその書を目にしては、心を新たにしている。その貫く棒の歴史とは、とりもなおさず武道の歴史でもある。

棒術についてまず知っておいてほしいのは、「武の神髄は柔体術であり、武器の主体は棒と石である」ということだ。すなわち柔体術を基本とする棒術こそ、武道の原点なのである。そ

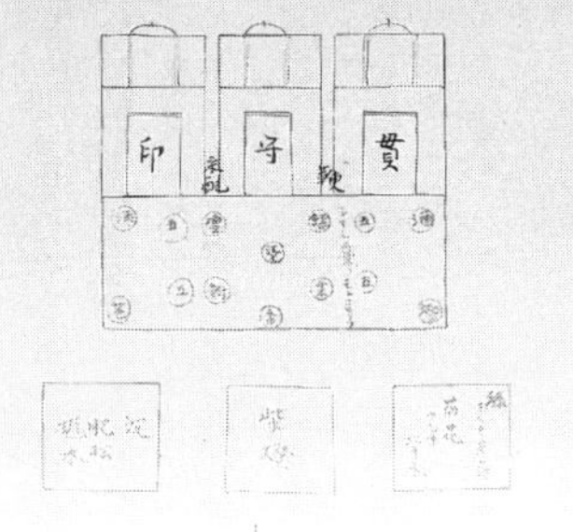

して武の神妙の真意とは「真に耐える」ことである。ちなみに、耐えるという音は、多得(たえ)る、即ち多くを得ると聞こえる。それだけに、武道の骨子は身体の構であるのはもちろんのことだが、その構を支配するのは精神であると肝に銘じてほしい。

まず柔体術が基本であり、それが身についてはじめて棒の使い方がわかるものだ。棒術でも剣術でも一番大切なのは柔体術。この柔体術ができなければ、棒のうまみ、味は出ず、棒の使い方に有効価値が生まれてこないのである。

私が師伝された伝書には、「最古の記録にては、兵法とは打拳法体術、棒術、剣術、弓馬術の、この五法を指して兵法と言っている。これをもって国を定め安んじ身を守ると言い伝えたのであった」と記されている。

また、昼の天と夜の天を表す「二天一流」で知られる宮本武蔵についても、こういう記述がある。「宮本武蔵は二刀流剣術のみの如くいわれているが、武蔵流棒術あり。武蔵流打拳体術の如きは一派をなして明治時代まで伝え残されている。かくのごとく古来の武士は、武芸中兵法はもとより築城、剣、槍、体術、馬術、棒術等も、誰でもが心得ていた」。

有名な巌流島の決闘で宮本武蔵は、小舟の櫂で削った木刀で、物干し竿と称された三尺余りの長刀を巧みに操る佐々木小次郎を、一撃のもとに倒した。武蔵は二刀流剣術ではなく、必殺の棒術の技をもって、雌雄を決するこの戦いに挑み、難敵の命を奪った。

一方の佐々木小次郎は昔習い覚えた小太刀の技の心得を求めず、物干し竿に心を奪われ、己の年齢を忘れてしまったのである。読者はもっと、考証家の世界と小説家の世界の時差を知らなければ、武道のエピソードを正しく理解することはできない。

武芸十八般という言葉の通り、武蔵は十手術、杖術、弓術、薙刀術など、さまざまな武芸の達人であった。従って、生命を賭した決闘の場で必ずしも剣をもって戦う必要はなかった。

武道では、禅の影響もあって、よく「身を捨てろ」とか「裸になれ」「無になれ」などと言うが、武蔵が剣から離れることができたというところに、小次郎に勝った秘密が潜んでいた。武蔵は剣からも、そしてまた女からも離れられたのだ!

しかし、じつはこれは一面では淋しいことであり、わびしいことでもある。なぜならば、人の歴史は(一)神話に始まり、(二)もののあわれの時代、(三)わび、さびの時代、(四)いき、いなせ、(五)みえの江戸時代を経過し、そしていまや(六)みえみえの時代、に入っているからである。日本の歴史を形成する、この六世代の潮流を見つめることによって、私たちは武蔵像、とくに吉川英治が描き出した武蔵の世界について再考する機会を与えられるのである。

棒術の種類

棒術には、手の内に入る短い棒から、八尺棒と呼ばれる長い棒(八尺とは限らない)を駆使する六尺棒術がある。

なぜ六尺と呼ばれるのか、それを説明する前に、まず知っておいてほしいのが、宮本武蔵の「五輪書」の書名にも用いられている「五輪」の意味である。五輪とは、地水火風空であり、それは木火土金水の五行ともつながるものであり、また五道=悟道、五術、五教であり、仁義礼智信の五常でもある。このように五というのは、多種多様なものの総合、統括を意味する重

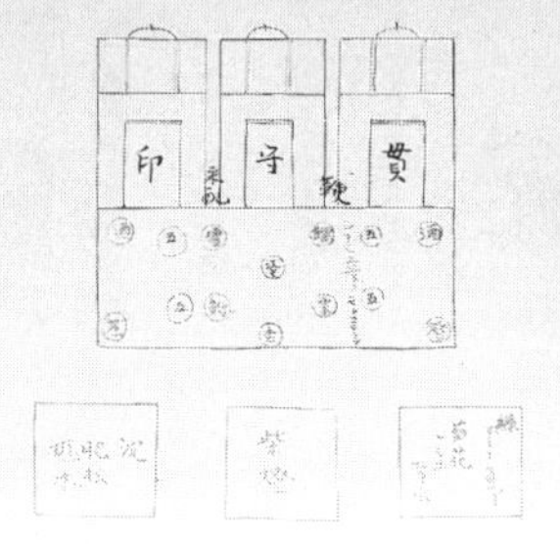

要な数である。

密教では、その地水火風空に、さらに識をプラスする「六大」を実体としている。いうなれば六尺棒術も、六尺という実際の長さではなく、この六大を意味しているのである。従って棒術の種類も、この六大を「霞の法」として、六つの六界から見るべきものだ。ここで山中に住んで、不老不死の法理を会得し、不思議な術を駆使すると言われる、役行者をはじめとする仙人は、木の実も口にせず霞を食って生きていたという譬え話に耳を傾ければ、棒術で言う霞の法も、実は道の教えであり、肝心要の六法全書をもたなければならない、ということが見えてくるであろう。六を知らなければ「禄(六)をはむ」こともできず、「ろくでなし」(六でなし)となる。

半棒術にもいろいろな技がある。たとえば、柳折という名の技は、次の通りである。胸をとって敵が襲う。左手で敵の右手を表逆にとり、右手にもった棒の先で敵のアゴを打つ。敵の右の脇の間に棒を入れ、敵の右の腕を折りながら、投げて捕える。

六尺棒の代わりに杖を使う杖術もある。樫の木やビワの木などを用いる棒術および杖術は槓技(かんぎ)とも呼ばれ、たいてい四尺五寸ほどの将軍木(赤樫の木)を用いた。槓技の根本は、変に応じ、機に臨み、虚につけいることであった。人が人を打とうとすれば、まず馬を打ち、その虚につけいって人を打った。

杖は「尉」の音に通じる。老人が杖をつく姿を思い浮かべれば、能の世界において、老翁の幽玄の世界ということになる。また「情」の音にも通じる。武士の情の「情」だ。すると杖術とは情実でもある。

棒や杖は、刃こぼれする刀にくらべて強靱であり、実戦の場で棒や杖が刀を叩き折る例もあった。また殺傷を避けようと思えば、それを可能にする護身の具でもある。棒の中には、如意棒のように、敵の鎧甲や、敵が乗っている馬の脚や背を打ち砕いてしまうものもあった。

棒や杖は敵を打つだけでなく、前方に障害物などがある場合、飛越にも力を発揮する、重宝なものであった。

また、棒や杖は、古来から神官などによって祭祀などに用いられる、宗教的シンボルでもあったことも見落としてはならない。モーゼが敵に棒を投げたところ、蛇に変じ、それを見た敵が逃げ去ったエピソードもある。

「棒」という字をよく見てほしい。「木を奉る」と書く。棒の本質は祈りにもつながるのだ。植物の中でも木はとくに空中のたくさんの炭酸ガスを吸収し、それを酸素に変えて吐き出すという、人類および生物たちが存続するための大きな働きをしている。まさに偉大なる転換である。木をもって棒刀にした意味がそこにある。

棒術の歴史

さて、棒術というのは、いつごろから発生したのだろうか。古伝には、根の国の野良で、素戔嗚尊が大国主命をためすため、大国主命の四方にある枯れ草に火をつけたところ、大国主命は一本の棒を拾って、この火をなぎたおして火勢を防いだことが記されている。また、出雲武命が三尺の「棒刀」で敵を倒した説話も残されている。この棒刀とは支配者しか所持することのできないものであった。刀剣の技法、そしてまた居合術、薙刀術、槍術などの技法は、こ

米 麦 粟 小豆
大豆 松 緑
蓬 菖蒲 菊花
沢 肥松 榧木
餅土 塩海 栗小 鮒
潮
北斗水
第一願主浄衣
第二七度禮拜
第三水印結曰誦文
第四護身法
第五九字
第六六根清浄祓
第七守尊之誦文
第八正命之誦文
第九拜眞之劍取三度
第十供奠之獻取
第十一祈現之扇取三度
第十二柴燈
第十三守尊之誦
テ唱テ祈也
敬禮退下
第十四當流祖師拜禮
東方構寶劍奉懸守印貫

の棒刀のテクニックから引き継がれて後世に成長したものであろう。棒刀には三尺くらいの、その地の強い棒などが用いられ、柄の個所だけを削ったという。

九鬼神流に残る記録によると、太古時代には三尺五寸の「刀棒」というものがあり、片方に石輪が嵌めこまれたり、八尺の棒の両端にそれ相応の石輪がはめられていて、これで敵の頭を打ち砕いたと言われている。

後世になり、刀棒や八尺棒の術が上手になるにつれて、その石輪がはずされ、刀棒は三尺くらいになり、半棒の術や棒刀術や杖術へと進化していったのである。もちろん八尺の棒も石輪がはずされ、六尺棒の術が生まれた。

古い棒術の流派としては神伝流、馗神(きしん)流、熊野流、九鬼神流、八方流、高木流がある、と記されている。

後年、諏訪流の流祖にして一刀流の達人である方波見備前守の伝書の記録によると「槓技(かんぎ)の法、一撃必殺を生む」とあり、この槓技、棒術についての説明が残されている。

私の流書には延元3年正月、足利尊氏(1305–58)が京都を攻めた際、官軍の結城親光の家来・大国太郎武秀なるものが、足利軍の豪傑・八代権之守氏里と一戦を交えた様子が記されている。戦国時代末期には、折れた矢の伝説のごとく「槍折の術」という棒術の名前も残されている。

また一方では、記紀や古伝では「棒刀」といわれるくらいであったから、「剣法を会得するには、三尺の棒刀の真理を会得しなければ、その理、計れず」ともいわれている。

九鬼神流棒術の歴史

九鬼神流棒術では次のような史実が伝えられている。――

延元元年(1336)、足利尊氏のために後醍醐天皇が花山院に幽閉されている折、楠木正成をはじめとする南朝の忠臣たちがなんとかして天皇をお救い申し上げなければと思案している際、紀州の行者の一人、薬師丸蔵人もその席に座していた。そこで、忍びの法を会得している蔵人が武勇にも優れているということで、この大任を命じられた。

その時、蔵人は16歳の美少年であり、蔵人は御殿女中に変装して花山院に忍び込み、天皇を背負い奉り脱出せんと廊下つたいに忍び足、しかし運悪しく雑兵どもに発見されてしまった。

気合いもろとも、天皇を背負うまま門前まで飛び降りるものの、四方より侍大将はじめ、武勇の者に囲まれてしまう。蔵人は木陰に天皇をお降ろしするなり、薙刀片手に、大将は誰か、と叫びながら斬り込んでいけば、雑兵草行くごとく、蔵人行けば倒れ伏していった。

がしかし、大将はさるもの、蔵人の薙刀・荒波の切っ先を逆に斬り飛ばす。「したり」と蔵人は六法九字霞の法にて奮戦、大将を打ち倒すところに楠木正成の軍勢が駆けつけ、天皇をお救い申し上げたのであった。

棒の稽古法

棒の稽古法として、型を正しく練習することも大事であるが、それ以前に柔体術の修行をおこたってはいけない。

棒術は、突き技を大事にすることが多い。極意の唄に「棒先で　虚空を突いて　我が手先手答えあれば　極意なりける」とあるごとく、虚空菩薩（棒察）の“仏怪”を悟らなければいけない。正しい突きを会得するためには、柱に五寸釘を一寸さしておき、釘の頭に向かって棒で突く訓練を続けることだ。霞を突き心を突くのも、虚空の一手である。

はじめは釘が飛んでしまうことが多いが、柱に釘がささっていけばOKである。次に体で突き、体で引く。このとき、棒を掌の中で強く握ることなく、宙で踊らせる。自由に繰り出し、繰り引くというより、遊泳させる。自分の体も同じくバランスよく遊泳させるのである。足も軽く飛び遊ぶよう心がけること。

敵に棒を撥ね上げられたり、剣を受ける場合でも、受けるというより振れ流す。そうしながら虚実（今日実）につけいり、敵の出鼻を撥ねる（「風姿花伝」の言い方に倣えば、「出花を散らす」ということになろう）、というような、パワーなき霞のごとき棒体一如の夢幻の妙実の会得に、一貫してほしい。

棒の木質（季質・気質）

棒術を修行するからには、棒の木質についても知っておく必要がある。木の質は育った環境などによって違いがあるからだ。あたかもたくさんの刀剣の中から正宗の名刀を探り当てられるように、すぐれた棒についての鑑定眼を養ってほしい。棒の木の種類は8種類ある。木本（基本）八法である。その中でなんといっても一番多く使われるのが、樫、なかでも赤樫である。常緑の大木であって、高さ20メートル、直径1メートルにもなる。自生する土地柄によっても強弱の特性があって、赤樫は、とくに堅く丈夫であると言われ、古くから武器の柄（つか）にも用いられていた。庭園樹や生け垣によく使われる荒樫は薄黒く、腐ったような色をしているが、非常に強い木質である。

樫の木には、白樫を含めて10種類あるそうだ。この10とは十文字であり、結ぶことを意味する。忍法体術で紹介した「十方折衝の構え」もここにつながっていることは興味深い。総じて樫の木は、9月の彼岸から12月の初旬にかけて伐ったものが一番よいとされている。寒中に伐ってもよいが、油がのっており、虫にたべられやすい。

樫の次にあげられるのが欅（ケヤキ）である。欅は木質が強く建築の構造材・装飾材や器具の材料に用いられる。杖、木刀、薙刀に使用するビワも強靱でよい。器具に用いられるモク（ムク、椋の木）も悪くはない。

そのほかの木を加工し、鉄のような強さに変えて用いることもあれば、鉄を素材とする棒、そして木の棒の中に刀を仕込む、仕込み杖もある。

このように、「弘法、筆を選ばず」の喩えのごとく、棒術においては一面では、木質を選ばぬことも知るべきである。

棒は木ばかりと思わぬこと

棒術の極意は、生き方の極意でもある。なんの変哲もない、たった一本の棒切れも、使い方によっては、いろいろな役目を果たしてくれるものだ。

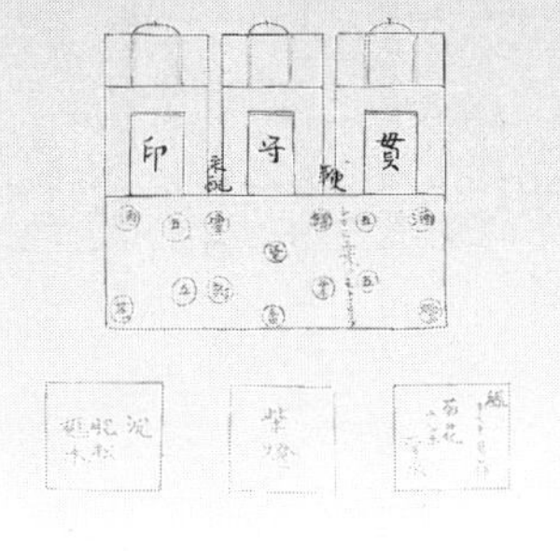

棒はどこにでもある。たとえば敵地に入るとき、棒を片手に忍び足で行けば、敵は明らかに攻撃にきたと判断するに違いない。ところが同じ棒でも、変装してこれを杖のかわりに持ち、足を引きずりながら行けば、おそらく敵はそれを見て、すっかり戦意を喪失してしまうであろう。怪我をしたと見せかけて猛攻を企てるといった、そのあたりの戦術は時と場合に応じて考えるとして、とにかく一本の棒も、ちょっとした頭の回転でいかようにも使いこなすことができるということだ。これは「詭変の棒」(敵を欺き変化する意。68頁参照)という名の棒術である。

相手が棒を怖がるようなときは、これをブンブン振り回すのも戦術のひとつだが、まったく無関心な場合は、いくら振り回しても無駄。自分が疲れるばかりである。

だから、心理的に相手の痛いところを突く――これも棒術の極意なのである。痛いとは「意多意」所、いうなれば「意識のある」所である。医学的、心理的にも「精神と肉体の痛み所」である。棒といえば、振り回す、突き進む、殴りつけるものだと思いこむのは、戦術を読むにも企てるにも、未熟にすぎる。

いろいろと複雑な現代だが、私はまっすぐな棒のように、素直に一貫する人間が好きで、そのように生きるべきだと主張したい。ところが、相手もつねに正直に接してくれるかというと、多分に疑ってかからなければならないところがある。

つまり、あなたが棒を使うときには、いわゆる表面的な棒の役目通りに使ってほしいのだが、相手が棒を持ったときは、はたしてそれをどう使ってくるかを考えなければならないということである。

相手が何かのきっかけで棒を引っ込めたとする。あなたへの戦意を失って引いたのだと、まず考える。ところが、そのとたん、あなたに大きな隙ができて、このときとばかり相手の棒がすっと伸びてくるかもしれない。それをやられてから、卑怯だと騒いだところで、後の祭りである。印象はどうであれ、そうなってしまうとあなたの負け、相手のほうが数段頭がよいということにもなりかねない。たとえフーテンの寅さんのように、できがよくないと自認する相手であっても、智恵を鼻にかけたり油断するようでは、とうてい敵わないものだ。

でくの坊(棒)、すなわち「手九の棒」(手は最高、九は技術を意味する)のように、社会的に、なんでもない人間のように見えても、辛棒一貫すれば、いずれは強い根棒(棍棒というより、この文字を用いたい)のような人物になるということだ。平凡な棒を修練によって使いこなすことができれば、平凡な人間が非凡なる人間になれる。ここに棒術の妙味がある。

武道の神髄は、見えないものである。単純にして平凡な武器を用いる棒術の稽古を倦まず弛まず続け、上達することによって、見えない超感覚の世界を超現し、心を洗い、すがすがしい精神の落ち着きを得れば、安らぎを覚える。しかも自信を得て、種々の恐怖心を無にする。武道の極意は棒術にあり、というゆえんである。

精神分析医かつ神学者のポール・トゥルニエ(1898-1986、スイス)は言う。「攻撃性はフロイトのリビドーと同じく生命力の一つの現れであり、その意味では誰の心にも潜んでいる」と。また、レイモンド・A・ダートも、こう述べている。「人類が類人猿の祖先から抜け出すことのできた理由は唯一つ、すなわち、殺し屋であったということである」と。ここに人間に潜む暴力性と武器の関係、そして人間の本質が鋭く衝かれている。

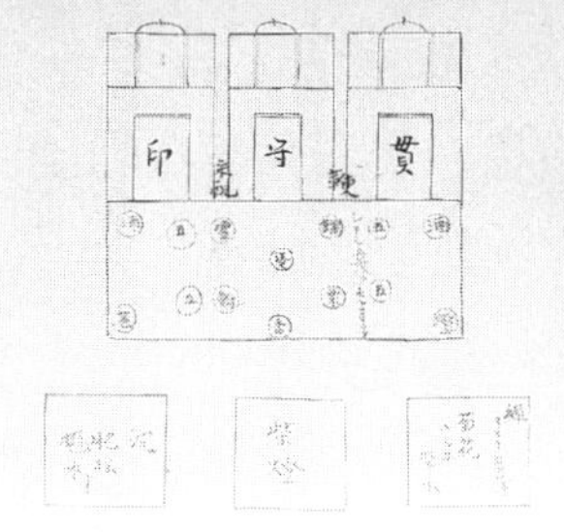

人類の歴史は500万年とも600万年とも言う。その長い自然淘汰（闘多）の歴史を、ダートの言葉を借りて一言で言えば、殺し屋だから生き延びたのだ。ならば今こそ人類は、応用自在の武器にして、かつ超感覚の世界への大道でもある棒術を学び、人類の闘争と殺戮の世界を生きながら、平安にして雄大なる、真の人間世界へと転換せねばなるまい。

TECHNICAL TEXT

棒の作法

左手にて棒の真ん中を持って歩む。相手と六尺の間隔で右手に棒を持ち替える。正座。一礼する。右足を半立ちと同じく棒を真っ直ぐに立てる。ここで相方（そうほう）は「お手やわらかに」と礼言を述べる。烈しく棒を前方に打ち倒す。右手にて棒を持ち上げ、左手を棒に添えて立ち上がりながら構える。

奇神九法の構

上段の構

棒の中心を両手とも下向きに握り持ち、両手の間隔は二尺とする。正しく左足の変化に備えて、軽く右足に重心を置き、左足前で右足は後方のこと。眼は敵の眼を見つめ、棒を頭上高く上げる。左棒先を敵の眼に付けるため、右の方が頭上で高く、腰はやや落とし気味に。脚を消す。浮渡りの構。

中段の構

棒の中心を両手とも下向きに握り、両手の間隔は一尺五寸程度。右　足を後方にして胸を張り、姿勢を正し、左手の方は真っ直ぐに、右手は自己の右乳の辺りに付ける。右足後方に重心を置き、右手の棒尻は地につける。楯に棒面を見せる。

下段の構

棒の中心を両手とも下向きに握る。両手の間隔は一尺五寸程度二尺程度。右足はややかがめ気味にして重心を置く。棒の中心を両手とも下向きに握り、左手は前方真っ直ぐに、右手は自分の横面に付く程度に。虎擲龍拏（こてきりょうだ）の構とも言う。

一文字の構

体は右横向きにし、顔は正面を向く。棒の中心を両手とも下向きに握り、両手の間隔は二尺程度。左右の足の間隔も二尺程度。棒をちょうど腰のところまで下げた構である。詞韻（しぎん）陰陽の構とも言う。

平一文字の構

一文字の構と異なり、体は真正面を向く。

譎変の構

譎とは、「あざむく」の意。すなわち、相手方をあざむき変ずる、という構で、左足前方、右足後方。両足の間隔は。棒先の面に隠れる。

青眼の構

右足は前方に左足は後方に置く。両足の間隔は一尺五寸程度。棒の中心を一尺二寸程度の間隔をおいて持つ。右手は左向きに左手は右向きにし、右手はちょっとたるみを見せ、鼻と直線一尺五寸の間隔になるよう右手を出し、左手は腹部に付く程度に置く。神心の構とも言う。

天地人の構

右向けの姿勢を取り、両足の間隔は一尺二寸程度。両手とも棒を自分向きに握る。棒の中心を握り、右手は顎の下に付く程度に肘を張り、左手は腹部に付く程度。手の間隔は一尺二寸程度。棒の中心を握るとはいえ上部に六分、四分が下になるようにして、棒を右横に構える。三略の構とも解す。

拳倒の構

この構は「払い」ともいう。左足は一歩前に出し、右足は後方に引き、両足の間隔は一尺二寸程度。両手の棒を二尺の間隔をおいて持ち、両手とも下向きに握る。右手後方に引き、棒は後ろ横にくる。この構は自分から打ち込むには不利であって、敵が打ち込めば決定的に自分の勝利となる。反応汎溢（はんのうばんえつ）の構と古伝される。

四羅起本型

受身

甲乙両人が道場の東西に相対し、一礼する。甲乙とも平一文字の構。互いの間隔は四尺程度。

一、甲は右足を一歩出すと同時に、右の棒先を乙の頭上に打ち込む。

二、乙は右足を左に一歩退き、右手の平で棒をはさみ持つ気持ちで棒を受ける。右手を頭より三寸程度のところに上げ、右手の肘は棒先の方へ。軽く使える左手は、左頭上左側に真っ直ぐに差し上げる。従って甲の棒が自分の頭上に来るが、はすになっている棒で、それを受ける。

三、こういう受け身のため、たとえ乙の武器が真剣であっても、棒を二つに切り離すことは困難である。右手の棒の上側に手の指が出ていないため、刀がすべっても指を切り付けられることはない。右手首より右肘までが軽く支えられているため、棒は受けに強い。体は充分そり身になっていることが大切である。

足払

一、前と同じく平一文字の構。甲乙の間隔は四尺程度。甲がまず右足を一歩前方に出し、同時に右手棒先で左足払い。このとき乙も甲同様に左足払い。しかし乙が後であるから、左足を引いて甲の左足払いと出る。互いの棒先が合致して打ち受けとなる。

二、甲は左手を放し左手棒先で再び乙の左足を払う。乙も同じく左手を放し、左手棒先で受ける。

三、そのまま甲は左手棒先で乙の右足払い。このとき棒は一寸左側にすべらすこと。乙も甲同様に右足を一歩引いて甲の棒を受ける。

四、甲は次に右手棒を左上部に放り上げ放す。その棒先が再び乙の右足を払う。乙もまた甲と同様にその棒先を受ける。

四方棒振型

棒の中心を左上向き右下向きに持って、右向け斜めに体をなして、右手の棒を下に押して、左手はうつむけとなる。同じく右手を下向きに握り、左手を放して体は左向けとなり、また左手下方に棒を押し、左手を放し右手が下向きになったとき、左手をまた下向きに握り、右手を上方に放り上げ左手が上向きになったとき、右手を下向きに握り、体をまた右向きとなして、前通りこれを繰り返す。すると棒は四方風車のような音を発して回るのである。右手の片手だけで回すことは、手棒では認められが、六尺棒では間違いである。

面打払型

甲乙とも右向けの姿勢で、棒は左手上向き、右手下向きに握り、甲は左手上部に放り上げ、左手棒先で乙の左足払い。そのまま棒先で左面を打っても、同じ型にすれば受け身となる。甲は左手の方へ棒を一寸すべらせて、そのまま乙の右足払い。また右手上部に放り上げて回し、右手棒先で乙の右足を払っても、甲と同じ型をとって受け身となる。

五境五界諷変捌型

これを霞の法へと転換する(25本)。さらに表裏一体とするとき50本とする。

五法

平一文字の構　一、左右に棒振り
二、右棒先で敵の左足を払う
三、右棒で左横面打ち
四、棒尻で右足払い
五、右に倒した棒先を回して敵右足払い

裏五法

平一文字の構　一、左右に棒振り
二、右足を引いて突き
三、棒先で左横面打ち
四、左棒尻で右裾を撥ね上げる
五、左手を放し棒を回して左面打ち

差合

中段の構　一、突き
二、棒を後ろにすべらして棒尾で左胴
三、左棒尻を回して下段撥ね上げ

船張

下段の構　一、右棒尻で左胴
二、棒尾で面
三、右足を引き右棒尻で撥上げ
四、棒尻で正面頭上に打ち下ろす

鶴の一足

天地人の構　一、棒を地に叩き倒す(これは敵の足を打つことである)
二、棒尻で左より両足払い
三、棒尻で右横面打ち
四、棒尻で天頭打ち
五、棒尻で左横面打ち
六、左手を放し左棒尻で左足払い

裏一足

下段の構　一、左裾払い

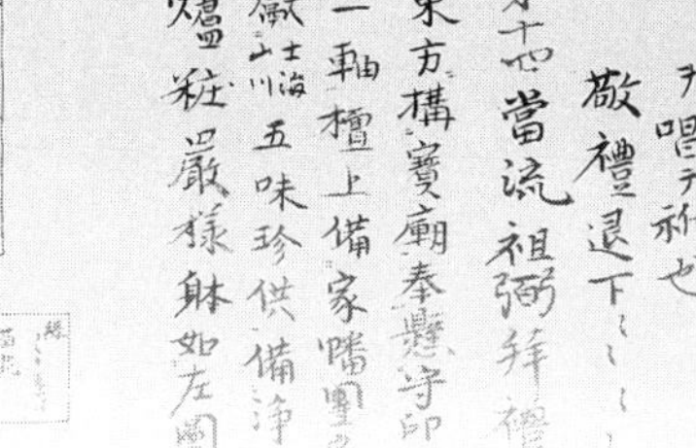

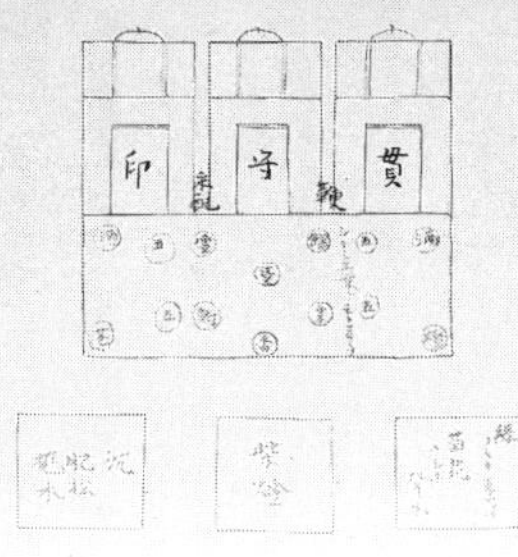

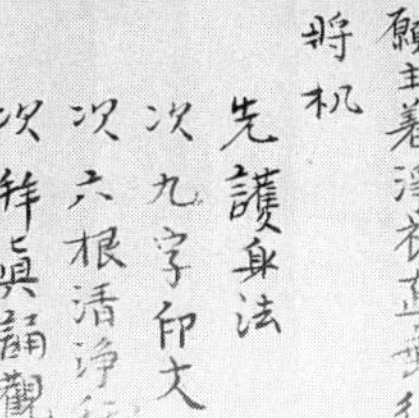

二、右裾払い
三、右手棒尻を放り上げて面
四、棒尻で天頭打ち
五、棒尻で左横面打ち
六、左手を放し左棒尻で左足払い
七、突き

裾落

中段の構　一、棒突き
二、左手を放し棒先で左胴
三、左棒尻でそのまま右足払い
四、右手上に棒を放り上げ天頭打ち
五、左棒先で撥上げ左足払い

裏裾落

中段の構　一、突き
二、左裾払い
三、右裾払い
四、左裾払い
五、右裾払い
六、右棒尻を放り上げ面打ち
七、突き

一本杉

天地人の構　一、棒を地に叩きつけ敵の足を打ち
二、一歩引いて棒尻で左足払い
三、左手の棒尻を上に放り上げ、回して右胴
四、そのまま棒尻で天頭打ち
五、一歩引いて右棒を放り上げて天頭

瀧落

中段の構　一、棒突き
二、左手より右肩に出て左横面打ち
三、小手を回し右手右脇より左肩に出て右横面
四、左手を放し右に撥ね左横面

虚空

中段に構えて突き。敵が右より左に打ち込むところを撥ね上げ、手元に飛び込み面打ち。
一、右足を引いて右手を折り左手高く受け
二、左足を大きく引いて左の棒先を回して左胴
三、そのまま左足払い

笠之内

青眼の構　一、そのまま右胴打ち
二、左足を引いて左胴
三、棒尻で下段から撥ね上げ

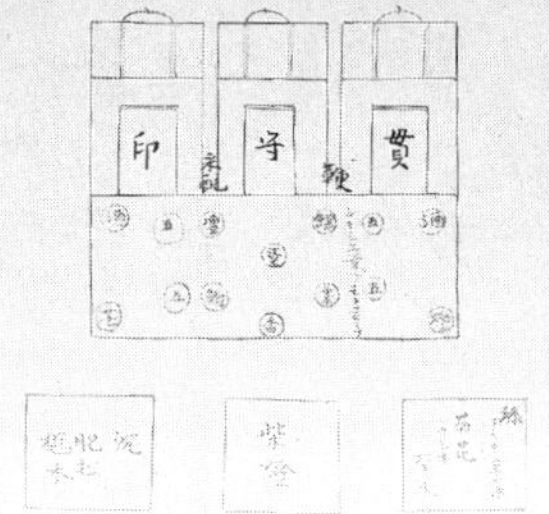

太刀落

一文字の構　　一、敵が打ち込んでくる
　　　　　　　二、左手を折り右手高く受け
　　　　　　　三、そのまま左足を引くと同時に右棒尻上から敵の小手に打ち下す
　　　　　　　四、左棒尻で左手を放し面打ち

払

一文字の構　　一、敵が打ち込んでくる
　　　　　　　二、左足を引き右棒尻上より小手に打ち下ろす
　　　　　　　三、敵の小手を左棒尻で撥ね上げる

小手附

中段の構　　一、突きに出る
　　　　　　二、棒を引き左胴
　　　　　　三、左棒尻を放り上げ面部に打ち込む
　　　　　　四、棒を撥ねて小手打ち

向詰

誳変の構（または鉾矢の構）　右棒を放り上げ面部に打ち込む。三度繰り返す

蹴り拳げ

誳変の構　右棒を放り上げ面部に打ち込む。五度繰り返し、五度目に左手を放し、放り上げ、蹴るごとく。左胴に打ち込む。

撃留

左青眼の構　　一、突き
　　　　　　　二、棒尻で横面打ち
　　　　　　　三、左足を引き棒尻で左突き
　　　　　　　四、棒尻を回して左胴

附入

右青眼の構　　一、左突き
　　　　　　　二、棒尻で胴
　　　　　　　三、棒尻を放り上げ突き・・・弯月(わんげつ)の構ともいう

五輪砕

左誳変の構（上蛇の構ともいう）　急所五輪とは「地水火風空」を指す
　　　　　　　一、棒を振り左胴打ち
　　　　　　　二、棒振り右胴
　　　　　　　三回繰り返す

天地人

天地人の構　　一、左より回し下段で撥ね上げて
　　　　　　　二、突きに変化する
　　　　　　　三、そのまま棒尻で右面打ち

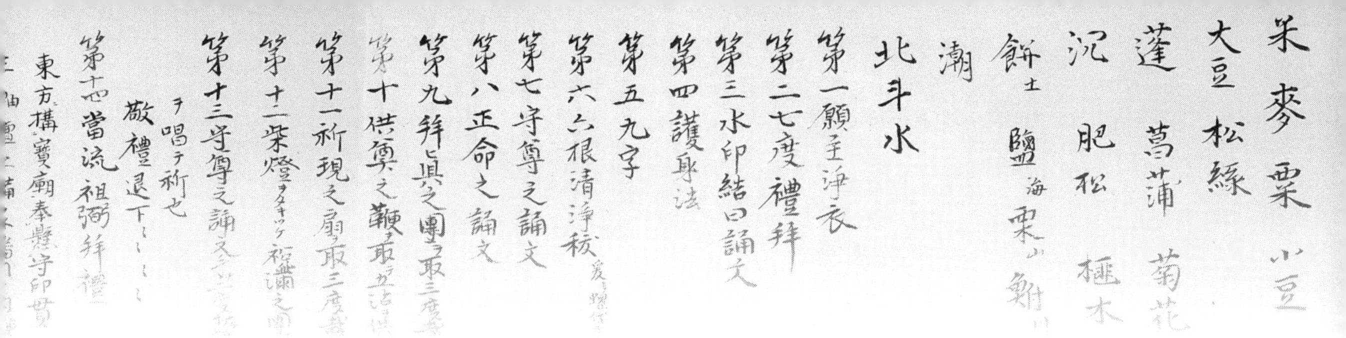

四、そのまま右足を出して左足払い
五、右足を引いて突き

前広

中段の構　一、棒尻で左胴に入る
二、棒尻で面打ち
三、一歩飛び退き一本形のごとく地に叩き伏せ
四、右足を床につけたまま突き

両小手

中段の構　一、棒尻で左足を引き両小手撥ね上げ
二、棒尻で面打ち
三、そのまま棒尻で下段撥ね上げ
四、そのまま棒尻で左足払い

浦波

譎変の構　一、棒突きに出て棒引き
二、棒尻を放り上げ頭部を打つ
三、棒を引いて突き
四、右手を放し左脇より後ろ胴に回し左胴に入る

玉返

譎変の構　一、面部に突き
二、引いて棒尻で左胴
三、左手を放り上げて左面部に突き
四、そのまま左足払い
五、そのまま左棒で下段

杖術

十文字

譎変の構　一、面部に突き
二、引いて棒尻で左胴
三、左手を放り上げて左面部に突き
四、そのまま左足払い
五、そのまま左棒で下段

六法

下段の構　一、そのまま体を回して左足払い
二、右手を放し放りあげ左肩にのせて棒を右肩より回し棒を取って左面打ち
三、左手を放り上げて突き

九法

中段の構　一、右下より下段撥ね上げ
二、左足を引き右棒尻で左横面打ち

田中又四郎
天保十一庚子年
二月吉辰

三、左棒尻で面打ち
四、棒尻はそのままに下段
五、右棒尻で左足払い
六、右手を放り上げ突き

飛龍

天地人の構　一、棒で敵の肩を打って
二、棒尻で面打ち
三、右手を放り上げ再び面打ち
四、左足を引いて左胴
五、左足を前進させ棒尻で下段撥ね上げ
六、左足を引いて左横面打ち
七、左棒尻で裾払い
八、左足を引いて左胴に打ち込む

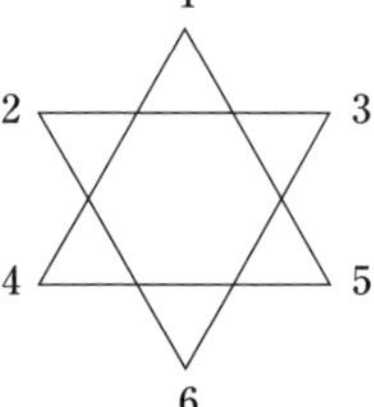

附入

中段の構　一、右足を引くようにして左棒左霞打ち
二、左手を放し左霞打ち
三、これを三回繰り返し、最後に面打ち

腕掛

文字の構　一、敵が太刀で斬り込む
二、左足を一歩引き、右手上、左手下にして
三、左手を放し腕に打ち込む

小手返

青眼の構　一、突きに出るのは虚
二、じつは小手を返して右胴に打ち込む
杖の場十体　㊉ 36度36体にて打つ。要するに九字数なり(○棒は円)

太刀落

青眼の構　一、面に出る敵を同じく面に来る
二、左手を引いて小手打ち
三、左足を地につけて下から小手で打ち上げる